do Pat Rice

**The**
**of**

GW00992849

*Pádraig Maolchraoibhe*
*Béal Feirste 4-3-2004*

# The Battle of Venezuela

**Michael McCaughan**

Latin America Bureau
LONDON

*The Battle of Venezuela*
was first published by
Latin America Bureau
1 Amwell Street
London EC1R 1UL
in 2004

Latin America Bureau is an independent research and publishing organisation. It works to broaden public understanding of issues of human rights and social and economic justice in Latin America and the Caribbean.

Editing: Jean McNeil
Cover Design: Diseño Atlántico, Buenos Aires
Interior design and setting: Kate Kirkwood
Printed by J.W. Arrowsmith, Bristol

A CIP catalogue record for this book is available from the British Library.

ISBN 1 899365 62 1

# Contents

# Acknowledgements

Thank you Lorraine and Yasmin for bearing with the distraction and dereliction of duty required to finish this book and to Stephen Mahony for abandoning his own projects to keep mine afloat. This book exists thanks to hundreds of Venezuelans who stopped to talk to me over the past five years, giving birth to a lively exchange of views and a number of valuable friendships. I haven't a hope of remembering all the names but a few spring to mind: Doris Theis, Augusto Montiel, Natali Vázquez, Francisco Prada, Leandro Area, Guido Zuleta, Zhandra Zuleta Castro, Carolina Troncone, Judith Galarza, Edith Gómez, Juan Vives and many more. A special thanks to the editors at Latin America Bureau, Marcela López Levy and Jean McNeil, for applying speed and rigour to the endless production tasks.

My investigation into the killings of April 11 2002 was made possible by Andrés Trujillo, who walked me through the massacre zone, Diogenes Lopez, Laura Salazar, Mohammet Merhi and Florangel Valdez.

Pemón leader Silviano Castro welcomed me into his community while documentary film maker Kim Bartley provided vital contacts and advice. Phil Gunson and Alberto Garrido patiently answered all questions but the conclusions reached in this book are entirely of my own making.

I have great admiration for Douglas Bravo, a veteran with five decades of selfless activism behind him. He spent many hours talking me through the past fifty years of popular struggle in Venezuela.

Enrique Vila kindly handed over the blueprint for a new Venezuela while government employees like Ana Lisa Osorio,

Zuli Hernández, Maria Urbaneja, Leonett Ricaurte and Jorge Giordani sparkled with enthusiasm despite the difficulties they face. Thanks to Alex and Gilberto and all the president's communication strategists, for the regular news updates.

In the barrios I found myself in the capable hands of Chuy and Elena, Cesar Azcanio, Ana Moreno and the mighty Coromoto, working night and day to turn Petare into a community based on solidarity.

Journalist Andrés Izarra was a breath of fresh air in a nation where journalists are expected to act as PR agents for big business interests. I owe a debt of gratitude to Carolina Hernandez Ponce for the emergency dental work.

Closer to home photographer Derek Speirs has been a constant source of wisdom and help, even outside office hours, while my family is there to answer every cry for help. Hail hail Caroline, Paul, Liam and Niall, the next generation. The Burren is my refuge and my inspiration where Steve and Dido, Chris and Sarah, Colin and Aine have reinvented the term friendship and a gang of children struggle to remain free in a society which will stop at nothing to tame them. Respect to Ramor, Ixim, Ana, Mike and Doris Archer, Danny Morrison, Christine Poland, Caoimhe Butterly, Erik Pedersen, David Gillespie, Heather, Roja Mhel, Ana Carrigan, Eamonn and Deirdre, Aoife and Suain, Tom and Susan, Adam and Emma, Bill and Emily, David Thompson, Barry Cooke, Jackie Bourke, Mairead, Matt and Yvette, Jarlath, Martha and Nick, Djennifer, Chelo, Una Ni Chiosain, Henry McLoughlin, Val Meikle, Luis Muñoz, Lupita, Pepe Gil, Rosaelba Arroyo, Alex Cox, Naomi Klein, Avi Lewis, Javier, Tatiana, Vicente, Elisa, Tiroteo and Luz, Alicia Malla, Veronica and Leo, Andrew and Gail, Rocio, Fr Shortall, Nuala Weber, Aldo Garcia, Jade and Saibhin, Micheal Fanning, Jenny McCrohan, Elizabeth and Joe, Eve, Dr Nightdub, Josephine Vahey, Monina Paz, Niall McGuirk, Yvonne Zimmerman, Dennis and Mary, John Jordan and the lovely ladies at Simon's Place, especially Simon. The soundtrack to this book was provided by

Eddie Vedder, Manu Chao, Ronan O' Snodaigh, Damien Dempsey, Rage Against the Machine, the Clash, Mike Scott and Sinead O'Connor. Joe Strummer, I miss you.

The *Irish Times* has continued to provide me with an important space in which to follow events throughout the Americas with Peter Murtagh, Paul Gillespie and Judith Crosbie lending an attentive ear to my wildest proposals. The phone calls connect thanks to Maureen and Brenda on the switchboard.

Anyone wishing to contact me can do so at the following email address: michaelmac2@hotmail.com

# Introduction

'If you seek vengeance, prepare two graves.'
Chinese proverb.

Revolutionary change is usually a matter of R-15s and M-16s, AK-47s and RPG-7s, but the main weapon in Venezuela's radical reform process is a small blue book that fits neatly inside your breast pocket. The book appears inoffensive at first glance, with the usual preamble on the rights of the individual, but read the fine print and you'll discover 350 articles alive with possibility, a cocktail of social and economic rights that promise a new society based on social justice and collective solidarity. And the beauty of it all is that this little blue book, Venezuela's new constitution, was passed into law by referendum in December 1999 without a shot being fired. Former United Nations High Commissioner for Refugees Mary Robinson described it as 'excellent' on a visit to Caracas in 2000, congratulating Venezuela for being the first country in the region to sign up to the International Court of Justice. However Robinson also sounded a note of caution, reminding Venezuelan officials that the calibre of passions driving such a dynamic process can easily turn into authoritarian sleight of hand.

Venezuelan President Hugo Chávez, the man behind the little blue book, wasn't always a firm believer in the ballot box. Years before his landslide election victory in December 1998 the former army paratrooper led a failed military uprising in

February 1992. But Venezuela's ruling class has also resorted to highly undemocratic tactics, turning to electoral alchemy and state repression in order to cling to power.

Some history is essential to understand Venezuela's current political standoff. A two-party democratic system was put in place in 1958 after squabbling factions united to overthrow an army dictator, Marcos Jiménez Pérez. The social democrats (*Acción Democrática*, AD) and Christian democrats (*Comité de Organización Política Electoral Independiente,* COPEI) shared the spoils of office and excluded the left from power, backed by the country's powerful business lobby which controlled the domestic economy. This arrangement found favour with the Catholic Church and successive US governments.

Venezuela is endowed with the greatest known oil deposits outside the Middle East, a key factor in mitigating the type of social unrest that has turned its neighbour Colombia into a deadly war zone for the past fifty years. The flow of black gold produced revenues that funded development projects and welfare programmes, trickling benefits down to the poor. In 1989, however, excessive borrowing and a drop in oil prices forced President Carlos Andrés Pérez to adopt an austerity package dictated by the International Monetary Fund (IMF). The result was a spontaneous social uprising which lasted five days, an orgy of looting only subdued by a punitive military expedition that left a thousand dead. These Caracas riots were the first major uprisings against an international trade accord, preceding the Seattle street protests by a decade. The nation's two-party system limped along for a few more years, but it was only a matter of time before someone harnessed the anger of the poor and created a new political movement.

Now, five years after Chávez assumed office, the social situation is still critical, a reminder that there are no magic solutions to deep-seated issues of poverty and injustice. Caracas, Venezuela's capital city, is literally falling apart as thieves filch metal from metro elevators, remove street lamps, dismantle apartment intercoms, steal electricity cables and pickaxe cement barriers separating car lanes on the city highways.[1] Residents' associations in upmarket neighbourhoods have responded by installing their own steel gates to illegally seal off their street from the outside world. In June 2002 I attended a security meeting organised by residents of Altamira, a prosperous Caracas neighbourhood. A strange, menacing mood had gripped this leafy suburb, beyond the everyday fear of kidnap, robbery and violence. This fear was driven by a seismic shift in social relations as the poor, invisible in their hillside shantytowns, came out of the woodwork and descended into the heart of the capital city. They came not to beg alms but to demand their share of the nation's wealth.

The Altamira security meeting took place in the patio area underneath the apartment block where I joined neighbours chatting about houseplants and hairstyles as they waited for a police liaison unit to discuss defence plans. The discussion had an air of unreality as the world outside carried on its usual lazy afternoon rhythm with teenagers sipping cappuccinos at the French bakery and garden hoses hissing over pristine lawns. My nearby fourth floor apartment was better protected than most European banks, an impenetrable fortress which would fall only to aerial bombardment. At the ground floor entry point two heavy security doors were followed by a lift which could only be activated by a secret code, taking you to a reinforced metal door with bolts and locks, all under camera surveillance.

An estimated 10,000 such residents' meetings took place throughout Caracas in 2002 as the middle-classes emptied gun shops and block-booked weekend sessions at the city's target ranges. Residents formed committees and identified doctors, and other professionals living in their apartment blocks who might be of use should the feared apocalypse come to pass. In the downstairs area of my apartment block a bulletin board listed recommendations for improving security, advising residents not to trust household help, as domestic staff returned each evening to their hillside barrios.

The blame for this anxious state of affairs has been pinned squarely on the broad shoulders of one individual – President Hugo Chávez Frias. All across Latin America the poor majority have been conditioned to view their social status as the inevitable outcome of a free, competitive society where winners and losers rub shoulders with no hard feelings. The occasional rags-to-riches story is presented as proof that anyone can make it if they combine persistence and hard work in a system based on equality of opportunity. The business sector creates the nation's wealth and jobs trickle down to the poor. Anyone who questions the consensus is quickly bundled out of the room like a naked man streaking across the stadium on cup final day.

President Chávez broke the unwritten rules of the political game by urging the poor to retake control of their lives and their country from the 'rancid oligarchs' who have controlled the country for the past forty years.

The nation's wealthy minority quickly struck back, accusing Chávez of riling the masses and bringing chaos to the country. Venezuela's mainstream media, a wealthy, private club with a virtual monopoly on national news coverage, have fabricated a version of reality that hungrily feeds and is fed by middle- and upper-class panic over the possible loss of their privilege and wealth. Business, media and displaced politicians decided that Chávez had to be ousted, by means fair or foul, to 'save' the country.

In ideal conditions Chávez's pledge to overhaul the nation's unjust system would be a daunting task: a five-year deadline to deliver peace and prosperity to 24 million people, 80 per cent of whom live in poverty. On top of this already herculean undertaking, Chávez has also faced three major blows to his plans: the devastating floods which struck in December 1999, killing 50,000 people and costing billions of dollars in reconstruction funds; the April 2002 coup; and a general strike which lasted from December 2002 until March 2003.

On my second trip to Caracas I booked into the Hotel Plaza Catedral on the centrally-located Bolívar Square. The owner was a dead ringer for the Portuguese writer José Saramago; tall, with sharp features, inquisitive eyebrows and an aloof manner that hinted at impatience beneath the polite exterior. I left my bags in my room and announced I was going to catch the final *Chavista* (as Chavez supporters are known) rally on the eve of the Constitutional Referendum in mid-December 1999: 'I'd cut his throat if I had a chance,' said Saramago, who began to froth at the mouth in an uncontrolled outburst of ill-temper. I stammered some neutral comment, explaining that I was a journalist, but the damage was done and he continued his tirade of abuse. From that moment on I was scowled at, messages were mislaid and visitors ordered to stay in the foyer lest they join me upstairs and declare a Bolivarian Circle. Three days later, relations with the hotel management had completely disintegrated and after a vicious row over unjust telephone charges Saramago called the stocky chef and ordered me out of the building. Within minutes the hotel hallway was bristling with aggression. I ranted at the management in Venezuelan gutter Spanish until Saramago, unable to contain himself, lunged at me, howling obscenities in a spitting rage. His son managed to restrain him and the standoff was resolved when baffled tourist police provided an armed escort to another hotel.

This was a shocking glimpse of the violence that lurks just beneath the surface of Venezuela's boiling social cauldron. If a hotel owner and a foreign journalist could reach an irretrievable breakdown in 72 hours, how must the rest of society be getting on as Chávez cracked open class divisions that represented centuries of social inequality?

## Note

1  *El Nacional* July 2, 2003.

# 1

## On the Campaign Trail – *a paso de vencedores*

Venezuela's 1998 presidential campaign trail was dominated by the towering presence of Hugo Chávez, who managed the remarkable feat of uniting all opposition candidates against him in a desperate bid to prevent him from winning office. The establishment favourite was Irene Sáez, a former beauty queen (Miss Universe 1981) who fancied herself a Latina version of Margaret Thatcher. 'I think she was right to introduce a market economy,' she said of her heroine. 'Right to reduce taxes, and tackle unions and privatise public services.' Sáez's impeccable teeth, strawberry lips and a halo of blonde hair marked her as a member of the upper-class elite, a privileged minority who jet to Miami for weekend shopping sprees, live inside gated communities and employ an army of servants to take care of domestic duties.

The greatest scandal on Sáez's campaign trail occurred when the ageing beauty queen, in an effort to assume gravitas, drew her hair back into a chignon and allowed it to grow back to its natural mousy colour. 'The people were in shock,' admitted Irene. 'I had done it Grace Kelly-style you know, but I had to change back.' Sáez used her unlimited access to radio and television to promote her campaign pledge, *'cambio'* (change), an appealing if vague promise to improve the country's ailing fortunes. The country's traditional parties, discredited by successive scandals, were heading for certain defeat. The left-wing Causa R (Radical Cause) backed Sáez's candidacy, a sign of the confusion that reigned in political circles. The upper-class favourite enjoyed 56 per cent of voter preference until Hugo Chávez's shoestring campaign picked up momentum through a series of rallies around the country. The media dubbed the contest the Beauty and the Beast, as a smiling Sáez waved the peace sign at television cameras while Chávez signed off with a clenched fist, phalanxed by supporters sporting his trademark red paratrooper beret.

This was no routine election to swap one set of grey suits for another: this was a battle for the very soul of Venezuela. Chávez promised a new constitution as a tool for restoring popular faith in a despised political system. There was talk of a 'third way', a rejection of left and right and a return to national development within the globalised economy. Chávez warned the oligarchy to prepare for radical changes and praised the poor for their patience in the long march toward social justice. A fervent Christian, he noted that God drove the moneylenders from the temple and hinted at a divine mission to rescue Venezuela from the autocrats who had bled the nation dry. The nation's powerful oil executives backed Irene Sáez, who promised to pursue privatisation plans for the key industry. Chávez steeped himself in the masses and marketed himself as the successor to independence hero Simón Bolívar, the great Liberator, who freed the country from the yoke of Spanish tyranny. Now, he said, there was a fresh tyranny to be overthrown: the neo-liberal nightmare which had impoverished the nation and concentrated power in the hands of a small business elite and their corrupt political allies.

Meanwhile, an embattled political class sandbagged itself behind sympathetic media coverage and a well-oiled electoral machine, both of which had guaranteed power for the previous four decades. This time, however the establishment defences faced a hurricane of unprecedented proportions. In an effort to limit the damage of a Chávez victory, the nation's congress sidestepped the constitution and called legislative elections a month ahead of the presidential ballot. The goal was to secure a safe congressional majority for the traditional parties and put a brake on Chávez's power should he win the presidency. The manoeuvre backfired and Chávez's left-wing coalition, Patriotic Pole (*Polo Patriótico*, PP) won eight of Venezuela's 23 gubernatorial elections, as well as 70 seats in the 189-member Chamber of Deputies and 18 out of 48 seats in the senate. Chávez's key campaign pledge was to rewrite the constitution and revamp congress, starting from scratch to rebuild the nation. 'Venezuela is a ticking time bomb,' warned Chávez, shortly after the elections, 'and I have been elected to defuse it.' [1]

In an effort to boost her withering campaign, Irene Sáez threw in her lot with the Christian Democrats (COPEI), who offered a lucrative war chest and a slick vote-gathering machine. The move proved a disaster, the death knell for a candidate who claimed to be an independent, beholden to nobody, ready to root out the corruption associated with the traditional political parties. In the final days of the campaign Sáez slipped into fourth place and finally pulled out of the contest advising supporters to back Henrique Salas Romer, another traditional politician recycled as an independent contender.

Pre-election polls revealed one telling detail about the evolving political process: a solid 26 per cent of those polled said they would vote for anyone *but* Chávez. This meant that one in four Venezuelan voters feared the rise of Chávez to the point where they would consider any alternative, however drastic, to prevent him winning office. In effect, the polarisation blamed on policies adopted once in office was already in place before election day.

It wasn't difficult to guess which section of society harboured fears about the charismatic rabble-rousing populist. The private media, controlled by millionaire businessmen, denounced 'the existence of arsenals and popular militias under the orders of Chávez.'[2] If Chávez won, the militias would become part of the government; if he lost, the militias would provoke civil war. No evidence was presented but the rumours persisted and were subsequently transferred to the Bolivarian Circles, the neighbourhood organisations set up in 2001 to strengthen government links to popular barrios. Venezuela's complete absence of media accountability allowed TV and radio commentators to mount a series of hate campaigns, each one more fulminating than the last, without fear of reprisal or even contradicting themselves.

In an interview published just before the election, Chávez outlined his future plans; 'First, a national constituent assembly, elected from all social sectors. It will establish a new and genuinely democratic constitution, political system and congress. We'll also attend, for once, to basic needs, like health care and education, and transform the current, brutal, neo-liberal economic model.' These campaign pledges could not be implemented under the existing state institutions controlled by the two dominant political parties.Venezuela's democratic structures rested upon a worm-eaten façade that housed a network of businesspeople, judges, lawyers, police, journalists, politicians, priests and soldiers engaged in a web of corruption and mutual protection.

'Venezuela is facing the most difficult challenge of young democracies; to build a structure of legal accountability for those in power,' explained Luis Moreno Ocampo, president of Transparency International for Latin America and the Caribbean. 'Whereas elsewhere such arrangements took centuries to achieve, countries like Venezuela must do it in a few short years.'[3] Ocampo's organisation had just ranked Venezuela as one of the ten most corrupt nations in the world.

It was widely reported in newspapers and television that Chávez had threatened to 'fry his opponent's heads in boiling oil' once he assumed office. The statement reminded me of Chilean dictator General Augusto Pinochet, who boasted of burying his victims two to a coffin to save on nails. In a region where the military uniform is associated with war criminals like Jorge Videla and Ríos Montt, the intemperate outbursts of army commanders who treat civilians like uniformed subordinates came as no surprise. The comments sounded plausible if suicidal for someone trying to win friends and influence people along the election trail.

Months later I discovered that the 'frying heads' outburst turned out to be the work of a talented mimic who was asked to record the memorable phrase for an advertisement, apparently unaware that the jingle would be appropriated for anti-Chávez propaganda purposes. Most Venezuelans are still unaware of the deceit.[4] Chávez's opponents lapped up every fresh scandal invented by the media while his supporters dismissed each new insult as the predictable reaction of a media empire beholden to the same interests threatened by genuine democratic reforms. The pattern would harden as time passed, making it extremely difficult to find a common language with which to initiate dialogue, let alone advance some form of negotiation. Both sides laid claim to two radically different versions of everyday events.

The Carter Centre, a US-based think tank established by former US president Jimmy Carter, recognised the significance of the 1998 ballot: 'This election could be one of the most important wake-up calls Latin America has had in years,' said Latin American director Jennifer McCoy. The US Government had denied Chávez a visa to travel there in 1995 and watched cautiously from the sidelines.

On December 6th 1998 the oligarchy's worst fears were realised as Hugo Chávez Frias strolled into office with 56 per cent of the vote, a stunning endorsement of the former coup plotter's alternative political project.

## Simón Bolívar

Simón Bolívar was born in 1783 into a wealthy Venezuelan family which traced its paternal roots to Vizcaya in northern Spain, although his mother was a *criolla* (of Spanish descent but born in the New World) with a hint of Indian blood. Simón Rodríguez, a talented educator inspired by French philosopher Rousseau, played a vital role in the boy's education; 'Instead of laying down the law,' Rousseau had written, 'let him obey the lessons of experience or impotence.' Academic advance was complemented by a regime of physical exercise, including survival skills, swimming and horse-riding. Another formative event was his witnessing at the age of twelve the execution of Jose Chirinos, who had led a revolt against Spanish rule. Rodríguez was implicated in the revolt and fled the country in 1797. Bolívar was dispatched to the army where his physical strength quickly earned him promotion and respect. When he returned to Caracas his uncles sent him to Spain where he moved in the highest circles as his protector, Manuel Mallo, was chief advisor to (and the lover of) Queen Maria Luisa de Parma, who dominated her husband King Charles IV.

Bolívar fell in love with Maria Teresa Rodríguez Y Alaiza, two years his senior, and married her while they were both still teenagers. The young couple travelled to Caracas in 1802, where Maria Teresa contracted a fever and died, just eight months after they had wedded. Bolívar was stricken by grief, and his natural idealism and romanticism dealt a lethal blow. He decided to devote himself to the liberation of a continent; 'The death of my wife placed me on the path of politics very early,' wrote Bolívar, in subsequent years, 'it made me follow thereafter the carriage of Mars rather than the arrow of Cupid.'

When Napoleon routed the Spanish monarchy in 1808, Caracas rebelled and Spanish authority came to an end as a junta was installed in 1810. Bolívar, who came into a huge inheritance on turning 21, financed and accompanied a delegation to seek support from Britain and the United States. Bolívar argued that the Spanish colonies should exercise self-government, a position rejected by the foreign powers but backed by his growing number of supporters at home.

The Spanish regarded the indigenous as subhuman and organised a system of economic exploitation which relied on terror and slavery. The Venezuelan economy, an early example of imperial protectionism disguised as global free trade, was impeccably defined by Bolívar:

> The Americans, in the Spanish system now in place, have no other place in society than that of simple consumers; even in this they are burdened with shocking restrictions, such as a ban on the cultivation of European fruit, with control of these products monopolised by the king, a prohibition on factories which not even the peninsula possesses, exclusive commercial privileges even over basic needs, and customs bans between American provinces so that they cannot trade, understand each other or negotiate. In the end, do you know what our destiny is? Fields in which to cultivate maize, grain, coffee, cane, cocoa and cotton; empty plains to create crops; deserts to capture fierce beasts; the depths of the earth to excavate gold which never satisfies this greedy nation.

At the battle of Carabobo, Bolívar crushed the power of Spain in Venezuela and established its independence, signed on July 5th, 1811. A new constitution in December 1811 declared federalism, liberty and equality, abolishing all distinctions between races, guaranteeing property rights and freedom of the press. In March 1812 nature conspired to deliver the cruellest blow yet to Bolívar's patriot soldiers, when a powerful earthquake shook Caracas and several other cities. An entire regiment of 1,500 independence troops fell into a fissure at Barquisimeto and were wiped out. Bolívar responded immediately; he was helping victims in Caracas when a pro-Spanish acquaintance came by, remarking that nature had put itself on the side of the Spaniards. 'If Nature is against us, we will fight it and make it obey us,' responded a defiant Bolívar. This famous quote, reproduced in a giant mural in downtown Caracas, would be resurrected by president Hugo Chávez during the catastrophic floods of December 1999.

By 1819, Bolívar had achieved one of the greatest exploits in military history, marching a ragged, starving army of 2,500 men dragging cannon and munitions from the steamy *llanos* (plains) of Venezuela over the barren, freezing peaks of the Andes into Colombia, a distance of almost one thousand miles. There, in the battle of Boyaca in August 1819, he engaged the main Spanish army of 5,000 men and defeated it decisively to break Spain's hold on neighbouring Colombia for good. Bolívar concluded his epic campaign in 1824, by which point he could claim to rule one of the greatest empires of any military leader in history: some three million miles, the size of eastern and western Europe combined. In ten years he had covered over 20,000 miles on horseback, fighting in some 300 battles and skirmishes. He dreamed of uniting all Spanish America under his rule, and wished to be remembered as a statesman as well as a military liberator.[5]

Bolívar's public appearances were greeted with wild applause and large crowds, culminating in the ancient Inca town of Cuzco, Peru, where he announced a land reform programme by which Indian farmers assumed possession of the land they cultivated and all communal land was to be divided among landless peasants. Bolívar was just 42 years of age yet the world, or at least the Americas, appeared to be firmly at his feet. This philosopher-soldier believed in a strong central state to guarantee the freedom of the weak against the strong, and an executive checked by parliament in consultation with the people. Bolívar also dreamed of a confederation of free Spanish American States. He liberated Bolivia, Peru, Ecuador, Colombia, Panama and Venezuela yet lived long enough to see the collapse of his life project. He marched through pathways of flowers strewn in his honour in all the capitals but refused the repeated offers of a crown to make him emperor.

In Bolivia Bolívar drew up a constitution which included civil liberty, freedom of speech, the press, work and movement, and equality before the law, as well as the abolition of slavery and provision for due process of law and trial by jury, described at the time as the most liberal constitution in the world. Yet he lived to see all his work come crashing down around him, only an instant after his dreams had become reality.

In the years following his military triumphs, divisions tore his achievements apart as one country after another succumbed to petty rivalries and feuding *caudillos*, the 'little generals' who ran Venezuela for the rest of the century. Bolívar retreated from public life, his health deteriorated and by 1830 he had reached the following conclusion: 'He who serves a revolution ploughs the sea.' He died, aged 47, in December 1830, penniless and almost friendless.

## Oil and caudillos

The nation's economic and social development shifted radically with the discovery of abundant oil reserves in the 1920s, a find that quickly transformed the nation into the world's second producer, after the US, and the world's chief exporter. The oil boom occurred under the iron-fisted rule (1908–35) of Juan Vicente Gómez, 'the tyrant of the Andes'. Gómez, like many leaders before him, was a caudillo. After Venezuela achieved full independence in 1819, twenty-two of its first thirty presidents were generals; and since then the country has had 25 constitutions and over one hundred changes of government.

The first oil wells went into production in 1914, and the vast natural resources of the country were discovered by Venezuela Oil Concessions Limited in 1922. Juan Vicente Gómez drafted the Venezuelan Oil Law (1918) which set aside half of all state-owned land with suspected oil reserves as 'national reserves', guaranteeing Venezuela's national interest. A royalty of 10–15 per cent was collected, either as oil, or its value in cash at contemporary world prices.

Gómez formed the Compañía Venezolana de Petroleo (Venezuelan Oil Company), with the dictator as principal stockholder.

No sooner were the maps of the oil concessions approved by the Development Minister than the reserves became the property of Gómez's company. Then, before any exploitation work was even begun on the adjacent oil sites, they were offered for sale. In most cases they were snapped up by the company that held the parallel concession, as that company had made the geological surveys of the land and knew its value. Within a short period of time the foreign companies owned the oil rights to all the land and there were no National Reserves left at all. By the late 1930s Standard Oil and Shell controlled 85 per cent of oil extraction in Venezuela.[6]

The oil industry grew in isolation from the rest of society as managerial and professional posts were almost entirely staffed by foreigners, while fenced-in oil camps created prosperous enclaves complete with private schools, roads, shops and health clinics.[7] With the passage of time the fences came down, but the oil industry remained a state within a state, retaining substantial privileges in relation to other economic sectors. Oil revenues made the state independent of society, thus strengthening authoritarian rule. Vast revenues were raised to pay for armies and bribe politicians without resorting to taxes or falling into dependence on foreign subsidies. The international community was pleased with Gómez, who repaid foreign debts on time – in fact the Papal Nuncio bestowed the Pope's award of Cavalier of the Order of Piana upon him.

Meanwhile dissidents were routinely imprisoned, tortured and murdered. The traditional agrarian oligarchy and the commercial bourgeoisie which once engaged in export activities now focused on urban commerce and property, paving the way for the powerful corporations of today.[8] A strong Bolívar (the national currency) raised the price of agricultural exports and reduced the prices of imported goods, a pattern which crippled domestic production and led to an overwhelming reliance on imported goods, even basic foodstuffs.

The oil boom convinced farmers to abandon their lands and migrate into urban areas ribboned on a narrow strip of territory from la Guaira to Puerto Cabello on Venezuela's northern coast. Nowadays almost 90 per cent of Venezuelans live in just 10 per cent of national territory, and 75 per cent of food products are imported, creating an unhealthy dependence on fickle food prices. The oil boom also resulted in a major cultural shift as rural Venezuela, once celebrated as a source of identity and inspiration, was replaced by an oil rush with its promise of money for nothing. Shiploads of tourists came to visit, thousands of emigrants settled in the country and foreign writers produced glowing accounts of the merits of the benevolent old dictator, basking in the apparent progress of the nation and the happiness of the people.[9]

A minor student rebellion in 1928 launched the influential Generation of 28, a group of academics who would later emerge as significant political figures during Venezuela's first attempt at creating democratic institutions. In 1935 Gómez died, and a brief period of democratic freedom began.

## General López Contreras: 1936–41

Gómez's chosen successor, General López Contreras, assumed the presidency. Immediately he released political prisoners and allowed hundreds of thousands of exiles to return home. Suddenly there was freedom of speech, of the press and of assembly. In a matter of months there were trade unions for every type of worker, even domestic cooks. However, Gómez's corrupt congress remained intact and the popular slogan became 'Liquidación' – total transformation. Media censorship measures were announced in February 1936 as the new regime, looking more and more like the old regime, showed its true colours.

A general strike was called. Crowds gathered outside the House of Government to listen to spontaneous orators. Army troops took up positions on the balconies of government buildings, aiming their weapons at the assembled citizens. A volley of shots was fired, causing chaos and a stampede which left eight dead and two hundred injured. López Contreras attempted to regain control, issuing the 'February programme' which promised widespread state reform by seizing the dictator's assets and squeezing the oil companies for a greater share of the nation's wealth.

The beginning of World War II highlighted the strategic importance of Venezuelan oil, and more favourable terms were carved out with the oil companies in return for an agreement to become a 'stable supplier' of oil to the US.[10] The emerging political opposition staked out new territory as nationalism, once regarded as the pursuit of national independence, now became linked to the struggle for economic independence. Foreign oil companies were held responsible for colluding with Gómez and providing him with the means to prolong his rule, provoking a popular backlash which drove the campaign for nationalisation of the country's most lucrative asset. Arturo Uslar Pietri, an upper-class intellectual, coined the historic phrase, 'Sow the oil'. The job begun by Bolívar was now seen as unfinished until the nation's subsoil had been reconquered and put to use on behalf of the people.[11]

## The birth of political parties

Acción Democrática, or AD, Venezuela's social-democratic party, was established in 1941. The two key leaders, Rómulo Betancourt and Raúl Leoni, missed the inaugural photo when the military authorities threatened to end the party if they dared to show up. AD quickly secured a nationwide support base with a multi-class membership, their rallying cry 'sovereignty, dignity and wealth' winning broad acceptance. AD founder Rómulo Betancourt wrote the party manifesto 'Plan Barranquilla' while in exile, outlining his vision of a 'national, democratic' revolution. The plan stressed the virtue of reform over revolution, as 'oil nationalism' would deliver wealth downwards to the poor without altering existing economic structures. AD dominated the nation's political life for the subsequent fifty years, taking power once by revolutionary means before winning six times through the ballot box.

Initial party progress was thwarted by the military, which held out against the introduction of universal suffrage. Impatient to seize power, Acción Democrática's leadership teamed up with dissident military officers grouped into the Patriotic Military Union (*Unión Patriótico Militar*, UPM), and planned a coup d'etat. The UPM and AD formed a tactical alliance and seized power in 1945 as the military rebels, led by Major Marcos Pérez Jiménez, pledged support for democratic reforms, installing a junta controlled by AD leaders, including Rómulo Betancourt and Raúl Leoni. Acción Democrática quickly revealed its skill at monopolising the levers of power, pushing its populist message with slogans like 'With AD you live better' and 'AD is the Venezuelan people'.

The Christian Democrats (*Comité de Organización Política Electoral Independiente*, COPEI) was born out of an ultra-nationalistic student group which aggressively opposed the left-wing tendency of Venezuela's Student Federation (*Federación de Estudiantes Venezolanos*, FEV). COPEI was formally constituted in 1946 under the leadership of Rafael Caldera, the veteran politician who handed over power to Hugo Chávez in 1998. The party's ideology was strongly influenced by the International Christian Democratic Movement, with family and civil associations deemed to play an important role in state development. COPEI was a conservative party which gradually shifted toward the centre in line with evolving church doctrine and the need to expand their voter base, concentrated in Venezuela's three Andean states. Rafael Caldera, COPEI's perennial presidential candidate, tried his luck in 1947, 1958 and 1963, winning 22 per cent, 16 per cent and 20 per cent of votes respectively. However the terms of the power-sharing arrangement worked out by the two parties, which would become known as the Punto Fijo Pact, enabled COPEI to join AD in a governing coalition under President Rómulo Betancourt between 1958 and 1963.

The two parties shared an aversion to class-based conflict and a willingness to compromise ideals to hold on to power. Caldera won the presidency in the 1968 elections by just 31,000 votes in a remarkable poll in which 97 per cent of the country's 4.24 million voters cast their ballots. Over two decades later, Rafael Caldera won re-election to presidential office, but even his venerable reputation failed to save the nation's sinking political structures.

Founded in 1931, Venezuela's Communist Party looked to the labour movement as the vanguard for change, and grew rapidly through it until the party was forced underground by government prohibition. Both AD and COPEI borrowed the 'Leninist' vanguard strategy to build the party infrastructure and mobilise support. Militants were dispatched throughout the country to counter the growing influence of the Communist Party.

When universal suffrage was finally approved, AD candidate Rómulo Gallegos – known simply as '*el maestro*', the teacher – stormed into office in December 1947, winning 75 per cent of votes cast. Acción Democrática promoted economic diversification and social welfare programmes, raising wages and subsidies for basic foodstuffs. The oil profits were also harvested within the party to boost membership and party resources, so blurring the division between party and state.

## 1948 Coup d'etat

In November 1948 a bloodless coup led by Delgado Chalbaud toppled the AD administration, reversing the process of political modernisation. AD was removed from power with barely a whimper of protest. The party had fought with the Catholic

Church over education reform and alienated rival parties through its clientelist approach to distributing state revenues and public service jobs. Gallegos accepted exile to Cuba while Betancourt headed for the Colombian embassy. There were no spontaneous protests, no strikes, no riots, no demonstrations and, thus, no repression.[12] While AD managed to enfranchise the masses, once in office it made no serious attempts at reforming the nation's unjust social order, and in the end the country decided it was easy to let it go.

## Army elections, 1952

The military regime felt confident enough to hold elections in 1952, relying on the junta's ambitious programme of public works and a tightly-controlled playing field: both AD and the Communist Party were outlawed, while Pérez Jiménez created the Independent Electoral Front (*Frente Independiente Electoral*, FIE) to square off against Jovita Villalba's Democratic Republican Union (*Unión Republicana Democrática*, URD).

The ploy failed, as early vote returns indicated certain victory for Villalba on election day in November 1952, throwing the junta into disarray. The military quickly annulled the vote and declared victory for Pérez Jiménez, prohibiting the publication of electoral results until the 'correct' result had been arranged. The US Government privately expressed its support for Pérez Jiménez, a critical factor in the junta's survival.[13] The US Government was grateful to Pérez Jiménez for rolling back any perceived communist threat and awarded him a special decoration, the Order of Merit, for his outstanding service to progress and civilisation.

Pérez Jiménez delivered the public works projects which became the benchmark for measuring the performance of governments ever since: agriculture was mechanised, dams and power stations constructed, railways and ports modernised and extended. Meanwhile 750,000 immigrants arrived from Europe, principally Italy, Spain and Portugal. The grateful immigrants displaced less-skilled local labour and provided political support to the regime. In return they were granted the right to vote after two years' residency in the country as Pérez Jiménez prepared the electoral terrain for a 1957 vote to ratify his regime's continued rule.[14] Pérez Jiménez's political prisoners suffered unspeakable torture: 'prisoners were slashed with razors, burned with cigarettes, forced to sit for hours on blocks of ice. Some prisoners were force-fed harsh laxatives and then, in a chamber of horrors awash with blood, excrement and vomit, they were forced to walk naked around a razor-sharp wheel rim.'[15]

Caracas city benefited from the dictatorship's building fever, fast becoming a glittering tourist and conference Mecca. Trade between Venezuela and the US expanded to reach US$1 billion in 1957 as Venezuela became the US's sixth-largest commercial market in the world.[16] 'Venezuelan law lets the foreigner operate freely, and US firms take their profit out in dollars, with no red tape,' gushed *Time* magazine. Strikes were forbidden and the trade union movement practically dismantled. The regime held a plebiscite in 1957, boosting their hopes of success by allowing only the participation of COPEI leader Rafael Caldera. Caldera refused the terms and was jailed, further isolating the regime. The plebiscite turned out a record 81 per cent vote in favour of the dictator, the final result announced long before the votes were fully counted.

On New Year's Day 1958 rebel air force planes bombed the presidential palace as the myth of Pérez Jiménez's iron-fisted rule crumbled in the face of popular resistance. Opposition was largely co-ordinated by the Junta Patriótica, formed in June 1957 by Fabricio Ojeda, a 29-year-old journalist and URD leader and Guillermo Garcia Ponce, a Communist party leader. The Communist party organised armed resistance led by Douglas Bravo, Teodoro Petkoff and Eloy Torres. The opposition demanded respect for constitutional rights and free elections and urged patriotic army troops to rebel against the dictator.

The plan was to combine a general strike with a military rebellion. Workers and students faced down the security forces on the streets with Bravo's group engaging in minor armed skirmishes.[17] A general strike paralysed Caracas on January 21st 1958 but the military lagged behind, only moving into action on January 23rd, the day that Venezuela's democratic system was reborn. Pérez Jiménez left for the Dominican Republic, taking as much of the treasury as was available in cash.

## From Punto Fijo to Hugo Chávez

The movement that toppled Pérez Jiménez was a range of interests, classes and sectors, united in their disgust at the dictator's arbitrary and personal rule. A five-man junta seized provisional power, led by Rear Admiral Wolfgang Larrazabal, who promised a return to constitutional rule and presidential elections within the year. The Communist Party threw its weight behind Larrazabal's presidential candidacy, resisting sectors within the party who pushed for a more radical assault on state institutions. Meanwhile the Junta Patriótica discarded the Communist Party to please the US Government and the private sector. Exiled political leaders were also anxious to curry favour with the US Government and peddled a conformist programme at odds with many activists who favoured more radical social reforms.

Popular feeling ran high against the US Government, which had granted refuge to the reviled Pérez Jiménez. When the then US vice-president Richard Nixon visited Caracas on May 15th 1958 he was received by an angry mob armed with sticks and stones. The city's municipal council declared the US politician *persona non grata* and the car in which he was travelling was smashed up. Nixon and his wife narrowly averted being dragged out into the street and beaten up.[18] Admiral Larrazabal said that if he was a student he would have done the same while the three centrist presidential candidates, Betancourt, Caldera and Villalba, all condemned the incident.

In order to prevent a repeat of AD's manipulation of power during the three-year democratic opening (1945–48), the parties agreed among themselves that the spoils of office would be shared among winners and losers. The Punto Fijo Pact, signed by AD, URD, and COPEI in October 1958, created a consensus system to ensure democratic stability. There would be a common economic programme and a 'spoils system' that provided for party control of appointments to state bodies, including the judiciary, military, electoral authority and bureaucracy. The church and military would retain their privileged position, the central role of private enterprise was written into the government's plans, and there would be no repeat of AD's attempts at educational reform, which had so alienated the church.

The Venezuelan Communist Party (*Partido Comunista Venezolano*, PCV) was excluded from the power sharing agreement, an act that formalised the process of exclusion which led the party to embrace armed struggle as an option of last resort to overthrow the system.[19] As a counterpart to political consensus, business and labour also signed up to a common programme, the *Avenmiento Obrero Patronal*, or Workers' and Employers' Agreement of 1958, in which unions traded restraint in wage demands for measures protecting job security and against unfair dismissal. A highly interventionist role was assumed by the state in the 1961 constitution, which included a raft of welfare provisions to minimise the prospect of class conflict. Oil revenues were to be distributed through the parties to their constituents and sectoral affiliates. Any organisation, from neighbourhood association to trade union, which did not associate with the parties was denied access to resources.

Acción Democrática candidate Rómulo Betancourt secured 1.2 million votes in the December 1958 election, ahead of Admiral Larrazabal who polled 900,000 votes, while COPEI's Caldera won just 420,000 ballots. In Caracas, however, runner-up Larrazabal easily defeated Betancourt and the election result was greeted in the capital city by riots and protests which lasted two days. Early the following year Fidel Castro made his first post-Revolution journey abroad to Caracas where an estimated half a million people greeted him with extended applause. Venezuela became an important focus point for the continental debate on the Cuban revolution with Caracas receiving the highest number of Cuban exiles after Miami, Florida. The exiles quickly established themselves in Venezuelan society, occupying important posts in the media and business world.

In the following years, inspired by the Cuban revolution, Venezuela's left turned to armed struggle but failed to win widespread support. President Betancourt survived his period in office but relied heavily on state repression. A peaceful demonstration by 50,000 unemployed workers in August 1959 was fired on by security forces and three people were killed. A few days later a student protest was attacked, with several more people killed. The repression led to a significant split within AD as youth leader Americo Martin resigned from the party and formed the Movement of the Revolutionary Left (*Movimiento de la Izquierda Revolucionaria*, MIR), taking with him an estimated 80 per cent of AD's youth wing. The expulsion of these factions deprived AD of a capacity to renew leadership and ideas. The *Miristas* also took 14 of AD's 73 deputies with them, fracturing their parliamentary numbers.[20] A period of popular discontent followed, with street protests crushed by troops who killed six, injured 71 and detained a further 500 people. President Betancourt blamed the unrest on 'high school students and boys without a trade or employment wandering around the slum areas of Caracas.'[21] The repression continued in 1963 when 1200 suspected communists were arrested and jailed, of whom 916 still awaited trial after 18 months behind bars. The government cracked down on opposition deputies, jailing Teodoro Petkoff and other communist deputies. A second split in the ranks of AD cost the party 26 seats and with them its parliamentary majority.

## Guerrilla warfare

If legendary British punk band the Clash had recruited a fifth band member in Venezuela, the dapper Douglas Bravo would undoubtedly have got the job. At seventy years of age Bravo still cuts a dashing figure as he roams the country, offering expert advice to communities in resistance despite the arrest warrant dangled permanently above his head. The son of a landowner, as a teenager in the 1950s Bravo joined the Communist Party and dreamed up an ingenious way to overthrow the state; rather than form a rebel army and wage guerrilla war, a lengthy and bloody affair with only a remote hope of success, Bravo persuaded his comrades to infiltrate the armed forces and get them to do the job instead. An estimated 80 per cent of army officers were drawn from the lower middle-class and peasantry, ripe grounds for Bravo's infiltration plans. [22]

Two hundred cadets soon waited for the order to rise up in support of an insurrectionary general strike. The moment never arrived, however, as the re-establishment of democracy in 1958, however limited, was greeted with relief after a decade of dictatorship. But the plotting continued as the Punto Fijo parties clamped down on peaceful dissent, provoking popular resistance. The first guerrilla attack came in April 1962 in Lara State; soon there were rebel fronts operating across the country, albeit with limited numbers and influence. The rebel leaders included Bravo and the Venezuelan contact for Che Guevara, who was of course planning revolution throughout the continent. The group also included Fabricio Ojeda, a URD legislator who played a key role in the patriotic junta which overthrew Pérez Jiménez and José Manuel Saher, son of an AD governor, who joined the MIR and took to the hills in 1962.

The rebel movement made little progress but in 1962 two navy uprisings brought new recruits to their ranks. In May 1962 a Venezuelan naval captain, with the aid of 450 marines, seized the Carupano naval base, announcing 'We can no longer ignore the countless abuses, arbitrary actions, murders and tortures to which our people are subjected.'[23] The uprising was crushed within 24 hours but June saw another rebellion, this time breaking out at the main navy base of Puerto Cabello, 70 miles west of Caracas. After two days' fighting – 'the bloodiest and most savage seen in Venezuela for years,' according to the *New York Times* – the rebels surrendered, although some escaped to the hills. Government losses were estimated at 200, with suspected rebel losses thought to be even higher.[24] In February 1963 the various guerrilla factions, including communists, dissident soldiers and independent militants, came together to form the Armed Forces of National Liberation (*Fuerzas Armadas de Liberación Nacional*, FALN). In 1963 the FALN carried out numerous actions, from the burning down of the Sears Roebuck warehouse in Caracas to the hijack of a cargo ship and the kidnapping of the deputy head of the US military mission in Venezuela. An assassination attempt on President Betancourt led to the total proscription of the Communist Party as candidates took to the campaign trail for presidential elections in December.

In spite of a rebel boycott, 90 per cent of citizens turned out to vote, electing Betancourt's successor, Raúl Leoni, who secured 32 per cent of the vote. President Leoni in turn handed over power to COPEI leader Rafael Caldera (1969–74), giving the appearance of a healthy democracy with transfer of power from one political party to another. The overwhelming consensus behind electoral politics proved a bitter setback for the guerrilla forces, who began to rethink their position and to consider re-entering the electoral arena. The communist party shifted its emphasis away from armed action and toward prisoner release, expelling Douglas Bravo in 1965 for criticising their retreat from armed struggle.

The death of Fabricio Ojeda in June 1966 was a major blow to the guerrilla movement as he represented the historic link between the struggle against the Pérez Jiménez dictatorship and the subsequent battle for participatory democracy and social reforms in the 1960s. The FALN struggled on until the outright collapse of armed struggle in the early 1970s. Bravo fought in the hills, was captured by security forces, escaped from prison and resurfaced in Paris in the 1970s, where he was – from afar – once more preparing cadres to infiltrate the armed forces.

## Chávez: origins and development

In 1980 Douglas Bravo finally hit paydirt when he recruited a young soldier named Hugo Chávez Frias, a member of the first generation of soldiers to benefit from third level education. Chávez was an enthusiastic conspirator who lapped up Bravo's wisdom then prepared his own 'Bolivarian' rebel movement, in honour of independence hero Simón Bolívar.

Hugo Chávez was born on July 28th 1954; his parents, both school teachers, encouraged his creative talents and he showed skill as a painter, baseball player and historian. The family traced its roots back to the nation's 19th century military rebellions, when Hugo's great-great grandfather was a guerrilla chief under Ezequiel Zamora whose 'Sovereign Army of the People' took on the landed oligarchy in the 1840s. The next Chávez generation produced Maisanta, a legendary figure who fought against the dictatorship of Juan Vicente Gomez in 1914. Maisanta married Claudina Infante, who had two daughters, one of whom, Rosa, was the grandmother of Hugo Chávez. As a small child Hugo heard adventure stories of epic battles and thrilling escapades, shaping his Quixotic vision of the struggle for a more just society. From his own grandmother he heard tales of Maisanta, whom the establishment dismissed as a bloodthirsty bandit. Chávez enlisted as a soldier in 1971 aged 17; three years later he visited Peru where he was impressed by the progressive ruling military junta led by General Juan Velasco Alvarado.

Venezuela's armed forces (*Fuerzas Armadas Nacionales*, FAN) developed in a manner different from their regional counterparts as periodic moments of national crisis have affected recruitment and membership. The War of Independence crushed the Spanish Army in Venezuela, producing a new generation of criollo caudillos who grabbed land and wealth for themselves. The Federal War in 1859 wiped out these leaders, giving way to an agrarian-based army with largely *campesino* (peasant) generals. In the decades that followed, a fresh clique of army leaders emerged only to be defeated decisively by Cipriano Castro in 1899, once more altering the composition of the forces. Castro sacked the entire officer corps and installed his loyal 'Andinos', who consolidated their presence under dictator Juan Vicente Gómez until they too were ousted in 1945 by Pérez Jiménez and Rómulo Betancourt. The joint army–civilian uprising in January 1958 led to yet another upheaval in the armed forces, while left-wing army revolts in the early 1960s prolonged the uncertainty.

By the 1970s the upper ranks of the army had been decisively co-opted into the bipartisan consensus, replicating the greed and graft that dominated political life. The Caracas riots of February 1989 and the twin military uprisings of 1992 once more upset the balance of power inside the army while the recent coup attempt against President Chávez (April 2002) led to further upheaval in the barracks.

'Once Venezuela found its first oil well,' explained Douglas Bravo, 'the bourgeoisie spent little time worrying about the FAN. They focused their energy on extracting as much wealth as possible from the oil, neglecting to organise the army behind their economic plans, as occurred in Colombia.'[25]

The great turnaround in the armed forces occurred in the early 1970s when the 'Andres Bello' plan was introduced, permitting troops to leave the barracks and attend universities to study sociology, engineering and medicine. The study programme endowed the military with the professional skills required to take an active role in nation-building. A new type of soldier returned to the barracks with professional skills,

civilian contacts and a fresh, social sensitivity, in sharp contrast
to the neo-Nazis flexing their muscles in the armed forces of
Argentina and Chile. That tradition continues today. General
Raúl Baduel, number three in the army hierarchy, is known as
'el Tao' due to his belief in oriental philosophy and meditation.
Baduel is against the use of weapons altogether, convinced that
positive energy is what counts on the battlefield. During the
failed coup attempt against Chávez in April 2002, Baduel
requested a megaphone rather than a tank when he declared
his loyalty to the President at the Maracay barracks outside
Caracas. Thousands of locals rallied to his side, camping alongside him in a show of civic-military solidarity.

Chávez contacted left-wing organisations that were gaining
ground rapidly in neighbourhood associations, student groups
and independent trade unions, an emerging civil society that
rejected the dominant political parties. In 1975, sub-lieutenant
Chávez received his sword of command from the hands of
President Carlos Andrés Pérez, the man he would attempt to
overthrow sixteen years later. As a young graduate from the
military academy, Chávez was dispatched to his home province
of Barinas, joining a counter-insurgency battalion which was
sent to Cumana to crush a bout of guerrilla activity in the area.
According to Chávez he began to sympathise with the left-wing
rebels while also noting the corruption around him as officers
fiddled budgets and inflated expenditure for personal gain. In
1977 Chávez gathered a handful of army colleagues to discuss
the possibility of radical change in Venezuela. He made contact
with key figures like Jesús Urdaneta Hernández and soon turned
his attention to forming a dissident movement within the armed
forces. Douglas Bravo discovered Hugo Chávez through acquaintance with his brother Adan Chávez, a university professor.

Chávez became a tutor in the military academy of Caracas
(1980–85) where the charismatic professor enjoyed enormous
influence over his admiring students. This period coincided
with a general disillusionment at corrupt, democratic institu-

tions and weak civilian leaders, and inspired Chávez to organise a serious military uprising. He created a secret cell within the
army, the Bolivarian Revolutionary Movement (*Movimiento
Bolivariano Revolucionario* 200, MBR 200), the number 200
marking the bicentenary of Bolívar's birth in July 1783. Chávez
launched the movement alongside Jesús Urdaneta and Felipe
Acosta Carles, the latter killed during the *Caracazo* (Caracas
riots) in 1989. The MBR-200 studied historic and contemporary
problems, recruiting young, discontented officers to their cause.
In March 1985 they were joined by Francisco Arias Cardenas,
a former pupil at a Catholic seminary who had many friends on
the left. However, military intelligence got wind of Chávez's con-
spiratorial activities and transferred him to an isolated outpost
in Apure province, close to the border with Colombia. In his
new surroundings Chávez emerged as a capable leader, co-ordinating civic-military projects and community events. Chávez's
quarantine period came to an end when he was assigned as an
aide to the national security council inside the presidential
palace in Miraflores, where he reconnected with his dissident
colleagues.

## The Caracazo

Venezuela's oil wealth produced an estimated US$300 billion
during the Punto Fijo years, (1958–1998) or the equivalent of
20 Marshall Plans. Despite the corruption and mismanagement
associated with the traditional parties, great strides were made
in literacy and welfare programmes, notably in the 1960s and
1970s, giving most citizens a minimal stake in the two-party
system. Venezuelan workers enjoyed the highest wages in Latin
America and subsidies in food, health, education and transport,
and this is the main reason why the guerrilla campaigns failed
to take off. The repression of the workers' movement and the
banning of the Communist Party significantly reduced the possibility of articulating an alternative political project but the

vast majority of citizens simply got on with their lives, content to knuckle under once they had food and shelter. By the 1980s, however, Venezuela's social contract collapsed under a tide of neo-liberal reform. Between 1984 and 1995 the percentage of people living in poverty jumped from 36 per cent to 66 per cent, while the number of people suffering extreme poverty tripled, from 11 per cent to 36 per cent. The worst single year for economic decline was 1989, when poverty rates climbed from 46 per cent to 62 per cent and the numbers facing extreme poverty more than doubled, jumping from 14 per cent to 30 per cent of the population.[26]

On the campaign trail in 1989, AD candidate Carlos Andrés Pérez denounced IMF economic recipes as 'la-bomba-solo-mata-gente', the bomb that only kills people, hinting that once in office he would pursue an independent economic path. The promise of radical social reform seduced left-wing parties, who threw their lot in with his candidacy. Soon after his inauguration, however, Pérez declared the Great Turnaround, embracing IMF economic recipes – supposedly to break with dependence on oil production and its fickle price fluctuations. In an effort to breathe life into the ailing system, Pérez granted ministerial status to a reform initiative called the Presidential Commission on Reform of the State (Comisión Presidencial para la Reforma del Estado, COPRE). Pérez also introduced direct elections of mayors and state governors and modified the electoral system for local authorities. Electoral abstention increased, however, another sign that Venezuelans wanted more than political reform if they were to have faith in democratic institutions. The adoption of IMF rules required the dismantling of welfare programmes, subsidies, price and wage regulations, with devastating consequences for the poor.[27]

On February 25th 1989 the government announced a hike in petrol prices, hitting Venezuelans not just in their pocket but also in their sense of national pride, as cheap oil had sustained a minimal sense of collective involvement in the nation's most lucrative public asset. Two days later a public transport price rise prompted university students, supported by workers and street vendors, to occupy a bus terminal. The protest quickly turned into a major social upheaval with barricades, road closures and looting spreading across the country. Passing food trucks were detained by protestors, their cargo unloaded and their vehicles parked across the highway. The security forces reacted slowly, lacking instructions from above as President Carlos Andrés Pérez, on a visit to another province, ignored the events, expecting them to fizzle out within hours. The scale of the Caracas riots took both the establishment and the opposition by surprise. The only organised group to participate from the beginning of the unrest was university students, who had been actively campaigning against neo-liberal economic policies over the previous weeks. The left-wing Socialist Movement (*Movimiento al Socialismo*, MAS) rode the wave of general dissatisfaction and achieved the 'great electoral leap forward' in December 1989, its candidates winning 20 per cent of the municipal vote – double that of five years before. The left also elected three governors, successfully challenging AD–COPEI hegemony over provincial states.[28] The MAS victory signalled a turnaround in left-wing politics as the party ruled out excessive reliance on mass mobilisations and entered the AD-dominated Workers' Confederation of Venezuela (*Confederación de Trabajadores de Venezuela*, CTV), arguing that the nation's privileged status as an oil producer translated into greater economic and political stability than elsewhere in the region. Graffiti began to appear on city walls bearing simple slogans: 'The people are angry' and 'the people are hungry'. A night of looting followed; the authorities watched, helpless, as a protest over rising bus fares turned into a major revolt. It was not until the following evening that President Pérez addressed the nation, appealing for calm while suspending civil rights and imposing martial law.

The army restored order by shooting hundreds of civilians, most of them in working-class districts. The final death toll has never been firmly established, but it is estimated that more than one thousand people were killed. On March 1$^{st}$, day three of the uprising, over twenty people were shot dead in the impoverished Petare area after troops opened fire on a group of unarmed civilians, and the exhumation of a mass grave in Caracas's public cemetery uncovered 68 corpses wrapped in plastic bags that had been secretly buried by the authorities. In the notorious 23 de Enero barrio soldiers tackled snipers positioned on rooftops while inexperienced recruits fired at buildings with automatic weapons, killing residents in their homes. President Pérez, who insisted that he had returned to office to seek his place in the nation's history books, achieved his goal, but not quite as he had hoped. His name is now ranked alongside Juan Vicente Gómez and Marcos Pérez Jiménez in the roll-call of national infamy.

## The 1992 coup attempt

In November 1991, Hugo Chávez and his dissident army troops advised their allies in the Radical Cause movement that revolt was 'imminent' and urged street action to support the rebellion. The *Causa Radical*, or Causa R as it is known, was a left-wing organisation which grew out of a split in the Communist Party and which had gained rapid influence. The movement directorate got cold feet and cancelled its support for the rebellion, fearing that association with a military uprising could damage its electoral prospects. But one faction of the party, led by Pablo Medina, continued to plot with Chávez. In January 1992 Medina met with Chávez to discuss a post-coup cabinet which would contain five civilians and four retired military officers.

In February 1992 Chávez and his rebel troops launched their military uprising. It was quickly squashed, with minimal loss of life. The only place in which the rebellion was a success was in Zulia state, where Francisco Arias Cardenas stormed government offices and took control of the local airport and the oil camps. One dissident soldier recalled how he had President Pérez in his rifle sights but hesitated for an instant and the moment passed. The promised civilian support did not materialise, deepening Chávez's distrust of the organised left. 'They knew but they did not arrive,' Chávez, said later, reflecting on the events.[29] In a dangerous foreshadowing of divisions ahead the ultra-left Marxist-Leninist party Bandera Roja apparently plotted to kill Chávez during the failed coup, giving rise to speculation that the military leader stayed away from Miraflores out of fear of an assassination attempt.

The government agreed to allow Chávez one minute on television to urge his comrades to surrender – a spectacular miscalculation on their part. Sixty seconds of airtime transformed the unknown soldier into a household name throughout the country. Chávez lamented the loss of life and took responsibility for the failed rebellion, but defended his goal of revamping the nation's moribund democratic system. He looked into the homes of millions of Venezuelans and announced he was putting down his weapons 'por ahora' – 'for now' – with the implicit suggestion that he would one day return to complete the task. In the 23 de Enero neighbourhood, named after the civic-military rebellion which secured the return of democratic rule in 1958, the residents cheered Chávez. And when Carnival began a few weeks later the most popular children's outfit was a military uniform with Chávez's trademark red beret.

The army upstarts were imprisoned while another coup, bloodier this time, and less popular, was attempted in November 1992, with disastrous results. Chávez remains unrepentant about the February 1992 coup attempt:

> Venezuela was suffering a terminal crisis, ruled by a dictatorship dressed up in democratic clothing, a dictatorship which took a people living on a sea of oil, with huge navigable rivers and millions of hectares of agricultural land, to abject poverty and limitless political and moral corruption.[30]

The gubernatorial and mayoral elections of December 1992 saw a decline in support for AD and gains for COPEI, Causa R and MAS. The two-party system enshrined in the Punto Fijo Pact had been fatally wounded. In 1993 President Carlos Andrés Pérez was impeached by congress for illegally using $17 million to support the campaign of Violeta Chamorro in Nicaragua and to finance his own lavish inauguration fiesta. An interim regime led by Ramon Velasquez oversaw presidential elections in 1993.

## Electoral alchemy

Venezuela's rigid political system, consecrated in the Punto Fijo pact, and its crooked electoral organisations played a crucial role in maintaining two-party hegemony. The presidential appointment of state governors, a situation which lasted until 1989, guaranteed a loyal nation-wide political machine. The system of 'block voting' in legislative assembly elections limited the choice of the electorate to a single list for the election of every official from members of parliament to parochial councillors.[31] The Organic Law of Suffrage also distributed election funds on the basis of results in the previous elections, guaranteeing a perpetual advantage to the vote-gathering machines established by the main parties. The Supreme Electoral Council (*Consejo Supremo Electoral*, CSE) relied on the Ministry of Social Affairs and the Immigration and Naturalisation Service to update the electoral register. An estimated 400,000 dead people were included in the electoral register as opportunities for fraud multiplied due to the partisan links between electoral authorities and party activists. The haphazard nature of building in the barrios added further opportunities for fraud while constituency sizes could be manipulated for electoral advantage. In a tightly contested area, militants could be registered to help gerrymander seats. The 1993 election results led to closer scrutiny of the CSE by smaller parties anxious to level the playing field. The La Causa R (LCR) delegate to the CSE found over 500 people registered as living in one house in Libertador district in Caracas while the Catedral district, with 4,000 registered voters, returned 16,000 votes in the 1993 poll.[32] A set of instructions issued to AD activists in Falcon state during the 1992 elections for governor offered a striking insight into ruling party tactics: 'When it comes to the military, try and win them with gifts, money and alcohol…. If necessary distract them with violence.' The Acción Democrática vote manipulation manual concluded with the following advice: 'Try and alter the ballot, particularly the vote of organisations with no witness.'[33] The CSE review of the 1993 electoral results proved a damning indictment of the system but the organisation ignored the findings, as reform would have endangered AD and COPEI's long-established winning electoral formula.

On the economic front, successive governments pursued a national development plan based on the import substitute industrialisation (ISI) programme, which combined state subsidies to domestic industry with tariff protection to punish competing imports. But access to credit, subsidies and markets were inextricably linked to favour with the ruling political parties, resulting in corruption and mismanagement of resources. The final outcome was the consolidation of large family businesses tied to the parties and the pauperisation of small and medium-sized firms. GDP rates grew by 36.6 per cent between 1961 and 1979, then contracted by 20 per cent between 1979 and 1990, as declining oil revenues led to international borrowing and a national debt that totalled $55 billion in 1990, soaking up a third of the state's annual budget.[34] The high income from oil had virtually eliminated tax collection, and citizens had come to expect free services in a country awash with oil money.

## Left-wing electoral alternatives: MAS and LCR

In the early 1970s, as the guerrilla war waned in the countryside, an opportunity arose for legal left-wing organisations such as universities, working-class neighbourhoods and trade unions to begin to press for change. A split in the PCV opened up debate as PCV leader Alfredo Maneiro criticised the party for failing to create structures and a strategy that would reflect the distinct flavour of Venezuela's popular struggle. 'No action, no success, no failure alters the structure, style or leadership. The party remains rigid and immutable,' complained Maneiro. By the beginning of the 1970s Maneiro believed that the armed struggle campaign had strengthened the flawed democratic system by offering a soft target for government repression and a pretext for curtailing civil rights to counter the 'Communist menace'.

At the 1970 PCV conference three rival currents emerged. A pro-Soviet 'right' squared off against a 'left' faction led by Teodoro Petkoff, with a 'centrist' group struggling to maintain unity. Maneiro's supporters attended a 1971 conference organised by the 'leftist' faction of the PCV at which the MAS was established, heralding a new era in Venezuelan politics. Maneiro's group dissociated itself from the new movement.

The MAS was allowed to participate in elections after the conclusion of a pacification campaign by President Rafael Caldera (1968–73), offering the first left-wing electoral alternative since a ban was imposed on the PCV during the 1963 elections.[35] The MAS believed that Venezuela needed an independent left-wing electoral option with a horizontal organising structure that would listen to the party's grassroots. While the MAS criticised the bureaucratic nature of the PCV, they immediately adopted a similar vertical organising structure. In subsequent years MAS has oscillated between 'euro-communism' and social democracy, its ranks occupied by the nation's intellectual class and its internal dissension dominating the country's political debate. The party's main spokesman was Teodoro Petkoff, a former guerrilla turned presidential candidate, newspaper editor and TV chat show host. Disillusioned by the Soviet invasion of Czechoslovakia in 1968 and weary of the guerrilla struggle, Petkoff moved steadily to the right, finally becoming Economy Minister in Rafael Caldera's second government (1994–98), where he was responsible for implementing neo-liberal measures.

Petkoff's predilection for allowing himself be guided by 'a strong moral sense of what it is right to do at any given moment'[36] accurately describes the party's shifting political allegiances. Nowadays MAS is split in two; one wing backs Chávez while the other wing is committed to ousting him from office.

Maneiro continued to search for an alternative organising model with a participatory grassroots structure. In 1971 the dissident communist formed Venezuela 83, linking two symbolic dates: the 200th anniversary of Bolívar's birth and the scheduled date for the termination of foreign concessions in the oil industry. The new movement hoped to harness the energy of civil society, acquiring a political identity along the organising road ahead. Venezuela 83 transmuted into La Causa R. La Causa R promoted the concept of radical democracy, a dialogue around the meaning of citizenship and sovereignty. 'The vanguard is not decreed, not conceived from above … but constructed from below with the people, from the people … without the presupposition of a specific party programme.'[37] The term 'radical', linked to peaceful yet revolutionary change, laid the ideological grounds for the emergence of Chávez's broad-based civic-military alliance. Radical Cause called for a constitutional assembly in the early 1990s and pushed the frontiers of national debate back to a time before AD and COPEI, rejecting left–right labels and appealing to the memory of independence heroes like Simón Bolivar. One of the organisation's core principles was the *encuentro*, a flexible meeting of equals which would engage civil society and build an autonomous but loyal support base. The encuentro was the principle underpinning 'radical democracy', defined as 'the maximum expression of individual sovereignty'.[38]

Venezuela 83 identified four points of confluence for its encuentro: two venues in Caracas, the Central University of

Caracas and the huge Catia barrio, were linked to with the intellectual community associated with the Universidad de los Andes in Mérida and the Venezuela Guayana Corporation, an industrial complex in Bolívar. The Catia 83 leg, renamed ProCatia, was the most successful: 20,000 signatures resulted in legislation that revoked the mandate of local councillors. The organisation's policy was to mobilise a popular social movement to achieve democratic change. The union wing developed an independent labour agenda known as *nuevo sindicalismo*, challenging the CTV's withered, ineffectual structures, which were entirely subservient to AD's electoral needs. Union leaders enjoyed wealthy lifestyles and were unaccountable to their members. The CTV leadership rejected industrial action in support of wage demands or improvements in labour conditions.[39] The legal framework allowed CTV executives to 'discipline' dissident unions and expel members from the confederation, while elections in federated union bodies could be annulled on demand. As an option of last resort the CTV maintained groups of armed thugs who imposed their will on recalcitrant workers.

Venezuela 83 leader Andrés Velasquez began addressing workers at the factory gate while a magazine, *Matancero*, brought the radical democratic message to a wider audience. The lobbying paid off, as Velasquez and the *Matancero* slate won the steel union SUTISS' elections in 1979, a victory which was annulled by CTV sleight of hand, with 3,000 employees dismissed as a reprisal. The Nuevo Sindicalismo continued to win fresh battles and by 1982 state security forces warned the government that the *Matancero* faction had reached the point where they constituted 'a real alternative to the traditional parties.'[40] The advice may have been premature, however, as the Punto Fijo chiefs still controlled the electoral machinery while the alternative parties lacked a significant national platform.

In 1978 Maneiro approached MAS and proposed an electoral alliance for future elections, but the offer was rejected.

The LCR then turned to José Vicente Rangel, a veteran left-wing politician; when he declined the offer to become presidential candidate, Jorge Olavarría, a supportive magazine editor, took up the post. The party was stunned by the death of its founder Alfredo Maneiro in November 1982 and the Olavarría candidacy came to an end amidst internal squabbling. Andrés Velasquez ended up on the 1983 presidential ticket but the voter response was negligible as LCR received just 0.5 per cent in congressional elections and Velasquez gained just 0.1 per cent in the presidential ballot.

By 1988, however, the party tripled its congressional vote and elected three deputies, while Velasquez won the governorship of Bolívar in 1989. The modest leap forward for the legal left was facilitated by the decentralisation process which ended the traditional appointment of governors and mayors, as these posts were put to the popular vote. The 1989 gubernatorial victories for MAS (Aragua) and LCR (Bolívar) provided the two parties with a national platform and increased media coverage. The following years proved a period of rapid growth for both parties, their participatory and anti-corruption message striking a chord with a people weary of graft and campaign lies. The local government reforms permitted alternative politicians to consolidate support in their home areas before challenging the two ruling parties on the national election stage.

Venezuela's debilitated traditional parties struggled to find ways to renew their shrinking influence in society. In 1983 AD's presidential candidate Jaime Lusinchi called for a 'Pact for a Social Democracy' which would launch a dialogue between civil society and the political parties. On taking office Lusinchi established the Presidential Commission on Reform of the State (COPRE), which brought a range of independent analysts together through discussion forums and seminars. The subsequent report recommended internal party reform, electoral reform and the decentralisation of political and administrative authority to directly elected regional and municipal executives.

Lusinchi's AD party shelved the report, ignoring its recommendations. [41]

In the years from 1958 to 1978 electoral abstention rates were among the lowest in the world, ranging from 6.6 per cent (1958) to 12.4 per cent in 1978. However, as the Punto Fijo pact proved incapable of opening up the electoral system to outside actors, abstention rates climbed steadily, reaching 40 per cent in 1993. [42]

## La Causa R in power

Andrés Velasquez, newly elected governor of Bolívar state, immediately set about demonstrating that another way of doing politics was possible: he removed 'invisible' workers from the state payroll, thus cutting expenditures by half, while implementing a breakfast scheme in 115 schools which covered 53,000 students, improving attendance and nutrition standards. [43] All LCR executives published detailed budgets which were drawn up in consultation with the communities involved. The organising strategy bypassed corporate media by pursuing low-budget alternatives like fliers, journals and mass meetings, combining information with internal feedback. LCR also placed full-page paid inserts into the national media, addressing their opponents. The 'adverts' attacked the CTV leadership and also challenged Defence Minister Admiral Radames Muñoz León after rumours circulated that the election would be cancelled on the pretext of uncontrollable mass demonstrations. [44]

LCR was also the only party in congress to oppose the IMF agreement in 1989, denouncing it as a betrayal of national sovereignty. The LCR experience in office was lauded as a model to be copied across the country, paving the way for a major electoral breakthrough in 1993. One drawback to the sudden rise of the LCR was that in their anxiety to offer candidates across a broad range of constituencies, the party accepted politicians linked to AD and COPEI, with some opportunists using the second wind to wipe their political slate clean. Other candidates had merely agreed to have the party register their names but never campaigned and did not expect to win many votes: 'I got a phone call on election night telling me I'd won a seat in parliament and would I please go to the count and defend my victory,' said Natalí Vázquez, a student activist who found to her surprise that she had become an LCR deputy.

## Caldera's last stand

As the December 1993 presidential election approached, the candidacy of Rafael Caldera, octogenarian founder of COPEI, began to gain legitimacy. Caldera represented moral security in a period of popular disgust with corruption and clientelism. His historic track record in combating authoritarian rule in the 1930s and 1950s left him uniquely placed to promise one last puff of oxygen into the Punto Fijo pact. COPEI, however, had other plans for the presidency, nominating Oswaldo Alvarez Paz, a move which led to Caldera's expulsion from the party. Caldera's exit from COPEI allowed him to organise a broad electoral alliance, *Alianza Solidaria* (AS) which incorporated dissident AD members and the MAS party, led by former guerrilla Teodoro Petkoff. The new electoral alliance attracted support from voters seeking an alternative to the AD–COPEI axis and offered the only opposition to the neo-liberal programme that appeared capable of defeating the two main parties. Andrés Velasquez, candidate for LCR, was a rising star but lacked the more moderate and higher public profile of Caldera.

By this time the nation's two-party system had reached exhaustion point. Hugo Chávez called for abstention, an option taken up by 40 per cent of the electorate. Rafael Caldera won 30 per cent, followed by AD candidate Claudio Fermin (23 per cent) COPEI hopeful Oswaldo Alvarez Paz (22 per cent) and, the real surprise, LCR candidate Andrés Velasquez, who polled 22 per cent of votes. It is widely believed that Velasquez's real vote was far higher but that victory was denied through fraud. The decision to enter parliament and allow the questionable presidential poll to go unchallenged disheartened activists and took the edge off the party's claim to a radical political heritage. These elections proved a watershed, as for the first time since 1958 the president belonged neither to AD nor COPEI, and their combined vote dropped from 93 per cent to 47 per cent.

Once in office, President Caldera lurched from one crisis to the next: a banking collapse led to a state takeover of the private banking system at a cost of $8.5 billion, or 75 per cent of the 1994 national budget.[45] The government then produced an orthodox stabilisation plan, Agenda Venezuela, in 1996, with a stand-by IMF loan worth $1.4 billion. The agreement paved the way for the opening of the oil industry to private investment which, together with an increase in oil prices, generated windfall revenue that temporarily contained social unrest. As fickle oil prices fell in 1997, however, Caldera prepared to sign up to an IMF shadow loan agreement the following year, acknowledging his post-election turnaround in a rare moment of on-the-record honesty: 'I had to take these measures because there is nothing else that can be done.'[46] In the late 1990s this political position was the norm in Latin America, where neo-liberal governments emphasised the 'inevitability' of the corporate global project, advising voters to get on board or face annihilation in the face of the oncoming economic juggernaut. One campaign promise which Caldera did honour was the pledge to release Chávez and other army dissidents who had been imprisoned since the 1992 coup attempt. They walked free in March 1994.

The LCR won 40 seats in parliament and a further eight in the senate in the 1993 elections, but the very success of the party distanced it from the grassroots as vertical power structures were replaced by bureaucratic machinery. The party took advantage of its numerical strength to forge a triple alliance with MAS and COPEI in 1995, raising LCR's profile on the long road to the elusive big prize: the presidency. The sudden access to power at the highest level resulted in a softening of the party's radical edge as the prospect of becoming serious players inside the political system led to the hope of even greater electoral gains ahead.

The organisation was thus obliged to assume positions which contravened its founding principles, and core voters began to see the party as simply another aspect of the rotten Punto Fijo system. The party remained divided between the more radical 'Medinista' faction, based around Pablo Medina, and the institutional Velasquez group, based around Andrés Velasquez. The latter faction was anxious to press home the party's electoral advantage. The demand for fundamental reform to the nation's political institutions was forgotten as deputies became absorbed in the daily routine of parliamentary horsetrading. The behaviour of LCR's congressional representatives contradicted the idea that the party offered an alternative to the status quo, while the encuentros lost their significance as a unifying, nurturing organisational tool. The LCR's control over one quarter of the seats in parliament left it with the worst of two worlds: the party could influence legislation but did not have the strength to impose its own agenda; the party helped prop up the discredited AD and COPEI parties and also gave the two-party state the appearance of political reform. The LCR paid the price in 1995, when a disastrous performance in local elections reduced party representation to one governor and a handful of mayors. The crisis brought the longstanding rivalry between Medina and Velasquez into the open with mutual recriminations over policy and tactics.

In an interview published in 1997, LCR leader Andrés Velasquez announced that he had been completely opposed to the two military rebellions in 1992, and that the party's ambiguous line on democratic rule had convinced the army to block the party from winning victory at the polls in the 1993 presidential contest. An ugly split ensued, with Velasquez's faction taking five out of nine senators but only thirteen out of 40 deputies. In April 1997 the electoral authority determined that the minority Velasquez faction was the real LCR and that group assumed the title LCR Velasquez. The Medina faction opted not to contest the ruling. The LCR pursued a moderate image and, lacking a credible candidate for the 1998 election race, opted early in the race to endorse the candidacy of Irene Sáez, at a time when she led the field by 20 points in late 1997. The LCR team joined Sáez's movement called 'Integration, Representation and New Hope' (IRENE) and in return Irene supported Velasquez's bid for the post of state governor in Anzoategui.

## Political allies

Meanwhile, Medina's group formed Homeland for All (*Patria Para Todos*, PPT) in July 1997 and prepared to contest the election on a radical platform for constitutional reform. The name represented the organisation's rejection of the neo-liberal agenda, which they believed undermined sovereignty and limited the national government's ability to determine the economic and political future of the country. The new party discussed the option of endorsing either Irene Sáez or Henrique Salas Romer, but both candidates were openly supporting free market reforms. The remaining option was Hugo Chávez, still an unknown quantity languishing at the lower end of the polls. His MBR 200 had opted for abstention in the 1993 national and 1995 regional elections, even though Francisco Arias Cárdenas, a coup colleague of Chávez, had registered for LCR and won the governorship post in Zulia state. Arias Cárdenas subsequently broke completely with Chávez and ran for president against him in July 2000, the runner-up with 43 per cent of votes. Chávez continued to meet with left-wing leaders as the Maneiro branch of the LCR inclined to support the prospect of a civil-military project. The LCR's ongoing, internal divisions led Chávez to distrust the option, despite the enthusiasm of Pablo Medina and Ali Rodríguez. Chávez was more attracted by the option of 'active electoral abstention' on the basis that the system would eventually collapse under the weight of popular indifference. However, the method proved too gradual to meet the challenge of the rapidly unravelling political system and Chávez's own thirst for power. At the MBR 200 national assembly in December 1996, militants voted to participate in presidential and congressional elections in 1998 and created a new movement, the Fifth Republic Movement, (*Movimiento Quinta República*, MVR). The new group would be a collection of movements striving to capture disaffected voters and generate a grassroots push to topple mainstream parties. The political platform would be necessarily ambiguous, allowing disaffected sectors to unite around a vaguely left-wing populist and nationalist project. The MVR harked back to the concept of the nation's 'three roots of the tree', namely Bolívar, Zamora and Rodríguez. The PPT voted narrowly to endorse Chávez in January 1998, concerned that the new organisation lacked the profile required to mount a serious challenge to the entrenched parties. While candidates did their best to maintain ambiguous pledges on the campaign trail, Chávez rejected the opening of the oil sector to private investment, while Sáez promised free market reforms and more privatisation. Six months later, Chávez had leapt into first place at the polls as a fresh economic crisis driven by a collapse in oil prices lent credibility to Chávez's platform for radical economic change.

On the campaign trail Hugo Chávez rejected this notion as a surrender of sovereignty and harked back to the idealism of Simón Bolívar, rallying the nation to a new political project, one that would redraw social, political and economic boundaries, paving the way for a Fifth Republic where citizens would enjoy equality and fair government managed by honest, competent *compañeros*.

On December 6$^{th}$ 1998, Chávez's dream of taking power became a reality. Supporters and detractors alike waited to see if the new president would fulfil his campaign pledges or suffer the same conversion to neo-liberal economics as his predecessors Pérez and Caldera. Chávez's governing coalition, the MVR, united genuine radicals with many opportunists seeking to hitchhike aboard the Bolivarian express to advance their own interests.

Chávez's winning Polo Patriótico alliance included allies in the MAS, La Causa R, the Movimiento Primero de Mayo, Patria Para Todos (PPT) and even ultra-left Bandera Roja, all anxious to assert their own identity within the new government.

## Notes

1   *Excelsior*, December 30, 1999.
2   *El País*, November 6, 1998.
3   *Time* magazine, August 23, 1998.
4   *Pagina 12*, December 18, 1998.
5   Harvey, R. 2000, *Liberators*. London: John Murray, p227.
6   Coronil, F. 1997, *The Magical State*. Chicago: University of Chicago, p76.
7   Ibid. p109.
8   Ibid. p87.
9   Ibid. p181.
10  Ibid. p107.
11  Ibid. p105.
12  Ibid. p143.
13  *New York Times*, October 12, 1955, quoted in Coronil, p156.
14  Coronil, 1997, p184.
15  *Time* magazine, August 23, 1963.
16  Coronil, p183.
17  Gott, R. 2000, *In The Shadow of the Liberator*. London: Verso, p123.
18  Ibid. p126.
19  Buxton, J. 2001, *The Failure of Political Reform in Venezuela*. Aldershot: Ashgate, p16.
20  Gott, p134.
21  Ibid. p135.

22 Bravo, D., Melet, A. 1991. *La Otra Crisis*. Caracas: Orijinal, quoted in Gott, p164.
23 Gott, p151.
24 Ibid. p153.
25 Garrido, A. 1999. *Guerrilla y Conspiración Militar en Venezuela*. Caracas: Fondo Editorial Nacional, pp14–15.
26 Ellner, S., Hellinger, D. 2003. *La Política Venezolana en la época de Chávez*. Caracas: Nueva Sociedad, p80.
27 Coronil, p375.
28 Latin American Perspectives, No 11, p140.
29 Buxton, p162.
30 Personal interview, February, 2002.
31 Buxton, p23.
32 Ibid. p88.
33 Ibid. p93.
34 Ibid. p40.
35 Ibid. p27.
36 Gott, p129.
37 Buxton, p137.
38 Ibid. p138.
39 Ibid. p41.
40 Ibid. p148.
41 Ibid. p43.
42 Ibid. p59.
43 Ibid. p153.
44 Ibid. p156.
45 Coronil, p381.
46 Ibid. p384.

# 2
# The Bolivarian Project

After his election, Venezuela's displaced political class predicted Chávez's speedy downfall and then set about fulfilling their prophecy. Former President Carlos Andrés Pérez bore a personal grudge against the new president, who had led a military rebellion against him during his second period in office. Even though he had been impeached for corruption, Pérez remained an influential figure and still harboured hopes of a political comeback. From his exile home in Florida, Pérez announced that Hugo Chávez wouldn't last a year in office. A few days later a group of retired army officers, the Institutional Military Front, publicly called on Chávez to resign. Venezuela's two-party hegemony dissolved, but displaced militants and politicians jumped on the Bolivarian bandwagon or reinvented themselves as 'civil society', loudly denouncing Chávez's political project as a 'totalitarian plot' to install communism in Venezuela.

While the defeated opposition licked its wounds and reshuffled its leaders, the permanent power behind the political system – the nation's business, media and church leaders – reluctantly opened their arms to Hurricane Hugo and his overwhelming popular mandate. Media moguls launched Operation Seduction to win the firebrand president over to their side, assuming that his radical rhetoric belonged to the hot air tradition of previous leaders who discarded populist pledges once they had served their vote-winning purpose. Venezuela's private television stations briefly courted Chávez on the assumption that, with the election campaign over, a moderate statesman would emerge from the ashes of the vitriolic coup plotter. It wouldn't be the last time the media confused its own desires with reality, badly miscalculating the national mood in the process. On the day after his triumph at the polls Chávez was invited onto one of the private TV stations for a lengthy interview in which a fawning presenter produced childhood photos of Chávez and invited a folk group to serenade the bemused president-elect. But the honeymoon would be short-lived.

Knowing they had been outmanoeuvred, the oligarchy tried to insinuate themselves into the president's inner circle. An emissary from the business sector approached him, offering 'advice' in the form of a list of recommended cabinet ministers. The jobs they wanted included the Finance Ministry, the Foreign Trade Ministry, various state-owned banks and the regulatory body for television and radio. The nation's business sector knew exactly what levers of state power it required to maintain its grip on the country. Chávez understood that his ambitious project would be best served by a constructive relationship with the nation's ruling class and accepted one of the business lobby's cabinet nominees, a decision he later confessed he regretted.[1] The elite remained on talking terms with Chávez for a while longer, but the symbiotic thread between the oligarchy and the political class had been severed, leaving the business, media and church hierarchies cut adrift from the evolving inner circle around Chávez. 'Chávez was elected in order to carry out the coup d'etat that he left unfinished in 1992, that is, to bury one political system and give birth to another,' wrote Raúl González, a member of a Jesuit centre for social analysis in Caracas.[2]

Within twenty-four hours of taking office, President Chávez signed a decree calling for a referendum to elect delegates to a constitutional assembly charged with writing a new national constitution. The new president also ordered troops out of the barracks and into the streets to repair roads and schools, distribute food and build health clinics under Plan Bolívar 2000, a strategy for welfare provision for the poor. Some 40,000 troops participated in the programme, which was designed to integrate the armed forces into the Bolivarian reform process.

## 1999 – reshaping the nation

In the early months of 1999 the mood on the streets of Caracas was euphoric as old and young alike discussed the Bolivarian project in shops and on streetcorners. Citizens eagerly debated the merits of embarking on a new political adventure which promised to improve living standards and forge an independent social and economic path toward some form of market socialism, guided by Simón Bolívar's vision of a unified nation led by a strong but compassionate caudillo.

Chávez short-circuited growing media hostility by demanding 'chain' time, a mechanism by which the nation's president had the right to sequester airtime on radio and television. In the absence of a media willing to transmit his views on the rapidly unfolding events around him, Chávez addressed the nation several times a week, sometimes speaking for several hours.

The constitutional assembly vote in July 1999 attracted over one thousand candidates, including gays, evangelists, firemen, artists, animal lovers, soldiers and singers. The result was another triumph for Chávez, whose slate of candidates secured 90 per cent of the vote, (with 54 per cent abstention) winning 126 out of 131 seats in the assembly. Among the defeated candidates was former president Carlos Andrés Pérez, who suffered the humiliation of failing to take a seat in his home state of Tachira. By mid-1999 Pérez had revised his prediction that Chávez would be gone by the end of the year, extending his survival period  by two more years. At that point, said

Pérez, President Chávez would be tossed out of power by an unstoppable popular uprising.

In a report on Chávez's first 100 days in office, the *Financial Times* of London noted that Chávez had 'begun to win the confidence of investors by presenting serious economic proposals,' and 'has launched a promising offensive on corruption and inefficiency and paved the way for a new constitution that is to allow for a more participatory democracy.'[3] Chávez pressed home the advantage gained from a landslide electoral victory, aware that his overwhelming mandate would fade quickly if he failed to lay the basis for long-term economic and political reform. The opposition was effectively locked out of the political process, a situation which suited Chávez's accelerated timetable for change but one which carried hidden dangers ahead. The *Economist* warned that Chávez's electoral success had given him 'an almost totalitarian grip' on the nation's democratic institutions.[4]

The Chávez slate for the constitutional assembly included his wife, brother, five of his ministers and several former coup plotters who backed him in 1992. It appeared that political loyalty rather than individual merit was the key factor in distributing posts. When it came to the re-legitimising elections for the revamped congress in July 2000 the pattern continued as retired military officers sought MVR support in 18 out of the nation's 23 states. The opposition hardened its attitude to Chávez and prepared for the war of attrition ahead.

The military influence has been a key factor in shaping Chávez's government since 1998, with cabinet posts and diplomatic missions distributed largely as rewards for political loyalty. Retired Air Force Colonel Luis Alfonso Dávila won a seat in the senate in the 1998 elections before being named Minister for Foreign Affairs in 2001. Chávez named Jesús Urdaneta Hernández, a founding member of MBR 200, as head of DISIP, the political police, an intelligence-based unit charged with detecting threats to the government, while general Arévalo

Menedez Romero, a colleague in the Military Academy, was named private secretary to the president. When Colonel Dávila was relieved of his duties at the Foreign Ministry it was Menedez Romero who filled the vacant post. General Ismael Hurtado was appointed Minister of Defence before Chávez appointed him Minister of Planning in February 2001, replacing General Alberto Esqueda Torres, who was posted to Brazil as Venezuelan ambassador. Military officers occupied top posts in oil giant Petróleos de Venezuela SA (PDVSA) while Admiral Hernán Gruber, another coup plotter, was named governor of the Federal State in Caracas. When Chávez was faced with a challenge to his authority by his army colleagues he quickly cut them down to size. After the Vargas floods in December 1999, human rights groups claimed that police units used terror tactics to control the civilian population, a charge rejected by DISIP chief Urdaneta Hernández. The DISIP chief demanded the removal of Interior minister Ignacio Arcaya and foreign minister José Vicente Rangel, but in the end it was the police chief who was ousted from his post.

The victorious constituent assembly declared itself the sole legitimate authority of the land, displacing the congressional deputies elected the previous year, and assumed the right to fire judges, mayors and governors. A *Ley Habilitante* (enabling law) issued 60 decrees allowing Chávez to fast-track legislation without congressional approval. It is not clear why the president picked a fight with the outgoing authorities, who would naturally have disappeared once the government set about revalidating institutions within six months. There was also a hint of mob pressure about the Chávez supporters, who jostled opposition legislators outside the congressional building where rival assemblies attempted to meet.

In August 1999 Cecilia Sosa, president of the Supreme Court, resigned her post and dissolved the nation's maximum legal tribunal, describing the move as 'a pre-emptive suicide to avoid being killed.' The move was reported as a blow to democracy and a clear sign that Chávez was engaged in the same brand of self-styled coup as Peruvian President Alberto Fujimori had mounted. The constituent assembly appointed a judicial emergency commission to investigate all judges with more than seven complaints against their work. The commission reviewed the work of 2,000 judges and court officials – out of a total of 4,400 – accused of corruption or ineptitude.[5] The judicial commission was made up of three representatives from the new assembly, one each from the supreme court and the judiciary council and three from non-governmental organisations. Opinion polls at the time revealed that 90 per cent of the population distrusted the existing judiciary. On the same day that Sosa resigned, eight of the fifteen Supreme Court judges voted to submit their posts to the constituent assembly, with only six in opposition to the move. In his best-selling book *¿Cuanto vale un juez?* (How much does a judge cost?) William Ojeda revealed the names of judges linked to government officials, business leaders, political parties and criminal interests. Ojeda was rewarded for his troubles with a lengthy criminal investigation and a one-year prison sentence. At his trial he was forbidden from calling defence witnesses and prevented from appealing to the Supreme Court for fourteen months.[6]

The nation's judicial system was overwhelmed, its prisons overcrowded and violent, a situation denounced repeatedly by Amnesty International and other human rights groups. In neighbouring Colombia – a country hardly renowned for its benign treatment of prisoners – the money spent per inmate was $316 per month, compared to a meagre $56 per month in Venezuela.

Despite the evident need for dramatic changes across a range of institutions, the opposition still denounced Chávez as an autocrat: 'Today there is a coup d'etat in Venezuela against the rule of law,' complained Timoteo Zambrano of Acción Democrática. Zambrano reinvented himself in 2002 among 'organised civil society' as leader of the Democratic Co-ordinator (*Coordinatora Democrática*), an umbrella opposition movement which demanded  the violent ousting of Chávez.[7] (In October 2003, Zambrano attended the International Socialist conference and tried unsuccessfully to secure the vice-presidency of the organisation.)

Over the following three months the constitutional assembly delegates debated submissions from hundreds of citizens around the country while President Chávez delivered his own constitutional text, which formed the basis of the new *magna carta*. The constituent assembly (*Assemblea Nacional Constituyente*, ANC) was presided over by the elderly Luis Miquilena, a surviving participant in the drafting of the previous constitution, in 1961. There were twenty-one commissions set up to debate constitutional issues, including citizen power, indigenous rights, sovereignty, economic issues, defence, education, health, the environment, human rights, women, sport, culture and justice.

The Catholic Church cried foul when news leaked that abortion might be permitted under some circumstances in the revised constitution. 'I knew something fundamental had changed when I heard the swish of cassocks and saw several bishops running up the stairs of the presidential palace,' recalled Maria del Mar, who sat on the women's rights commission. 'They would normally send their subordinates to dictate their orders.' In the run-up to the vote the church openly opposed Chávez. 'If the Yes vote wins then peace and democracy will be endangered,' said Bishop Roberto Luckert, who added, 'we may succumb to a constitutional dictatorship which is worse than a military dictatorship because he [Chávez] will have absolute power legitimised through the constitution.' Chávez was quick to respond, arguing that his enemies inside the church 'are on the side of the devil,' finishing with a quote from the Bible: 'Forgive them Lord for they know not what they do.'[8] The Catholic Church subsequently faced a cut in state education subsidies, a key factor in its enduring hostility to the Chávez administration.

The new constitution awarded unprecedented recognition of women's work in the home as enshrined in Article 88: 'The State will guarantee equality between men and women in the workplace. The State recognises work in the home as an economic activity which creates added value, wealth and social harmony. Housewives have the right to social security in accordance with the law.' The employers' federation Fedecamaras also complained bitterly about the new constitution, rejecting the principles underlying the economic chapter which stated that, while every individual had the right to protect their property, such rights were subordinated to the 'national good', rather than the 'general interest' as defined in the previous 1961 text.[9]

Venezuela's corporate media claimed that the new constitution aimed to curb freedom of expression, citing an adjective, which enshrined the right to *información veraz* or 'truthful information'. 'No one in Venezuela can trust Hugo Chávez's democratic credentials,' said Miguel Henrique Otero, editor of *El Nacional*, Venezuela's leading daily paper. Otero added that Chávez's efforts to hold the media accountable to the public masked his secret aim of 'controlling us, weakening us, neutralising us and turning us into accomplices of this governmental disaster.'

In any case, there was no fear of the national media going soft on Chávez; daily reports accused him of everything from wife-beating to global warming, the absence of effective libel laws giving free rein to the wildest claims. Meanwhile mainstream media owners laid down strict guidelines for their reporters, who faced dismissal should they contradict the anti-Chávez editorial line. President Chávez clarified his opinion on press freedom: 'I do not believe that any individual or watchdog group can determine if information is fair and accurate,' he said. 'It is public opinion which must make up its mind on each case.' The Bolivarian process encouraged citizen participation in all aspects of public life with particular attention to the media, a key player in shaping public opinion. If citizens felt misrepresented by the media then they were entitled to organise, protest and seek redress.

The role of the military in the 1961 constitution was defined as 'apolitical', but the new constitution gave the military the vote and allowed them to participate in politics with the rather vague restriction that they remain *sin militancia política* (without political affiliation) and followed the principle of 'discipline, subordination and obedience' (Article 328). The new constitution also ended parliamentary control over military promotions, which were now determined by the president and the armed forces themselves.[10] There was also controversy over the length of the presidential period and the possibility of re-election with one six-year period followed by one permitted re-election option. President Chávez, like all elected officials, would have to submit his existing mandate to a re-legitimising contest scheduled for May 2000. 'If the Venezuelan people decide that my time is up,' said Chávez, 'I'll abandon office without a whimper.'[11]

The constitution emphasised participation and protagonism, incorporating a series of tools to enable ordinary citizens to exercise direct influence over public affairs. Article 72 stated that 'all elected posts' from village mayor to president are subject to revocation of mandate halfway through the period in office. The petitioners must obtain the signatures of 20 per cent of the electorate if the referendum is to proceed. If the National Electoral Council (*Consejo Nacional Electoral*, CNE) validates the signatures, a vote is called. If the referendum is to be carried then the vote against the office holder must exceed the original vote in their favour. The revocation measures even allow voters the possibility of reversing presidential decrees, a move which requires an initial petition signed by 5 per cent of the electorate. The recall option empowered citizens to challenge elected officials who reneged on campaign promises or proved incapable of fulfilling their responsibilities. The 'protagonist' element of the Bolivarian process also offered citizens the opportunity to impose their will on elected officials. Article 70 opened up opportunities for citizens to introduce legislation or even constitutional reform, alongside 'citizen assemblies whose decisions will be binding' on elected representatives. Four years later, however, the legislation required to formalise the citizen assemblies remains blocked by anti-Chávez legislators.

A more straightforward mechanism for guaranteeing citizen participation in public affairs was also approved: a bill may be introduced to parliament by 0.1 per cent of the electorate, a move which allows 10,000 people to lobby parliament for legislative reform. A constitutional reform can be proposed by 15 per cent of the electorate. The president is entitled to call a constitutional assembly by decree while the national assembly requires a two-thirds majority to achieve the same goal.

The constitution offers tools for legislative reform and revocation of mandate, but the practical task of converting popular aspirations into legal action was contained in the enabling legislation subsequently approved by presidential decree. The *Ley de Tierras*, or Land Laws, state that anyone aged between 18 and 25 is entitled to a plot of land while labour legislation fixes the working week at 44 hours, with night time work cut to 35 hours. Such laws would come as some surprise to the workers in the bakery opposite my hotel, who work 7am to 9pm, six days a week, not forgetting an hour each way on the bus. 'My daughter hardly recognises me,' one woman told me, adding up her 84-hour working week. In interviews conducted with workers hostile to Chávez, the interviewees pointed to the ambitious promises contained in the consti-tution, interpreting the aspirations as immediate guarantees of health care, gender equality, free education, decent pensions, a home and an acre of land. The workers who supported the Chávez project invariably cited the promise of reform as a starting point in a long-term process that required energy and commitment to bear fruit.

Chávez and his political allies dominated the constitutional review process, but non-aligned civil society delegates also played a key role in preparing the final document. A series of forums, conferences and workshops by non-governmental organisations gathered 624 proposals for the new constitution, of which more than 50 per cent were incorporated into the document. Many NGOs and discussion groups were hostile to Chávez's political project but took advantage of the opportunity to shape the political map of the country. Organisations classified as 'neo-liberal' in outlook succeeded in pushing through a third of their proposals for the constitution. The success of autonomous organisations in influencing constitutional reform contrasted sharply with recent experience under the Punto Fijo system. After the 1992 coup attempts a constitutional reform process proposed 128 new articles, of which 28 were associated with civil society. Only five of the proposals were incorporated into the final reform project.[12]

Venezuela's emerging political order began to irritate the international media. 'Venezuelans overwhelmingly supported radical reform,' admitted the *New York Times* in an editorial, 'but they should be very wary of the methods Mr Chávez is using.' The editorial declared that Chávez 'has so far shown little respect for the compromises necessary in democracy.'[13] The *Times* didn't specify what sort of compromises it recommended in the pursuit of democratic ideals, but judging by its coverage of Latin America the editors seem to approve of compromises made on behalf of foreign investors and local business, the IMF, World Bank and other agents of global capital.

President Chávez was now making compromises on behalf of the poor majority, who were invisible to the media, their neglected rights ignored over the previous forty years. *Newsweek* magazine called time on Chávez's reform process, counting the 'victims' of his clean-up, notably Roberto Mandini, 'a widely respected free marketer' and head of the country's oil company, PDVSA. The oil executive resigned due to differences with the government over management issues. *Newsweek* then concluded that Chávez was going too far, citing sceptics 'from opposition politicians to American diplomats,' this apparently covering the entire spectrum of legitimate political scepticism. The constitutional commissions reported back to the assembly delegates who, together with legal advisors, drew up the draft which was put to the vote in December 1999.

On the eve of the referendum heavy rains began to fall. Chávez addressed a crowd of about half a million people on Avenida Bolívar: 'I will turn Venezuela into a first world nation within ten years', he promised, and the crowds danced and sang in the streets into the early hours. Chávez provided his usual dose of provocative vitriol, rallying the troops with fighting talk: 'Let the naysayers know we are just beginning our counteroffensive, we are going to unleash our forces on all flanks. The order is for persecution and relentless attack.' Chávez talked it up in front of his home crowd, a pep talk to boost the side for the final push before the referendum. To the opposition, however, each word was measured, debated and dissected for possible clues to future government actions.[14] Maria de Jiménez, a retired teacher who attended the Chavista rally, held her copy of the provisional constitution aloft: 'This is the best Christmas present we could have got,' she said, 'it's for my ten grand-children, not for me.'

The rains continued through the night, threatening precarious homes on the hillsides around Caracas, but no-one imagined the level of catastrophe about to befall the nation. 'I hope the rains continue so they don't come down to vote,' one well-dressed woman told me as she arrived at the upmarket Country Club booth where she cast her vote against the constitution. 'They' were the poor majority who live on the hillsides above the city. Some voters did defy the rains and turned out to support the constitutional reform package which was passed by 71 per cent of voters, with abstention at 54 per cent – heavy rainfall and perhaps the sense of foregone conclusion kept voters away. The voting pattern was consistent along class lines: in the wealthy neighbourhoods of Caracas the majority voted against the constitution; the more populous but less wealthy barrios voted overwhelmingly in favour of the document. In Miami, Florida, where thousands of exiles cast a vote at their embassy, 76 per cent rejected the constitution, a clear sign of the political leanings of Venezuelans living in the US.

Even as the votes were being counted, the news filtered in that neighbourhoods were beginning to flood and evacuation was urgently required. The Chávez administration abandoned celebrations and moved into emergency mode, mobilising troops and health workers to the affected zones. Death struck with characteristic indifference: in Naiugata district, Caracas, a school diverted an avalanche of mud and saved thousands of lives while a few miles away eight hundred people who sought refuge in a church were buried alive under several metres of mud. The floods cost between 30,000 and 50,000 lives as mudslides buried entire neighbourhoods and turned the centre of Caracas into a mudbath.

Anti-Chávez sectors pointed to the floods as divine retribution for the government's audacious attempt to alter the course of nature – rich and poor being viewed by the detractors as part of the natural order of things, and not to be stirred too much or risk explosion. History repeated itself as farce when the Archbishop of Caracas, Ignacio Velasco, blamed Chávez for the mudslides and ordered the St Paul of Nazarene statue to be taken out of the church and paraded through the streets, an old tradition reserved for 'great calamities'. Velasco pondered aloud to the crowded congregation: 'There are sins we commit which attract the wrath of God. Such is the case of "that man" who improvises and succumbed to pride.' Velasco then asked God to forgive Chávez his sins. 'Nature itself reminds us that we do not have absolute power,' he said, as the national anthem replaced the Gloria during the mass.[15]

A year after Chávez assumed office, social indicators offered a sober reminder that referenda, elections and debate do not put food on the table; an extra half a million citizens had joined the ranks of the unemployed. Foreign investment was on hold as businesspeople waited to see what way the new country's institutions would operate before committing their capital. Thousands of wealthy families voted with their feet and left for Miami, Florida, exactly forty years after thousands of wealthy Cubans departed Havana for Caracas, terrified at the triumph of Fidel Castro's rebel army. The exodus continued in 2002 as 43,000 Venezuelans arrived in Spain that year, and only 8,000 returned.[16]

## 2000 – the relegitimisation of new institutions

Now the Chávez administration had the constitution it had long dreamed of. The next task was to relegitimise every elected official in the country, from president down to community delegate. The opposition remained paralysed by the speed of events, lacking even a semblance of an alternative political vision. Mega-elections scheduled for May 2000 would elect the nation's president, state legislatures, city councils, mayors, governors and members of a new National Assembly. As the date approached the novice National Electoral Council was overwhelmed by the task of co-ordinating ballot papers for 35,000 candidates competing for 6,000 posts.

Meanwhile Venezuela's participatory democratic process had raised hackles inside the Clinton administration, where officials admitted to being 'exasperated' at Chávez's dedication to popular consultation. 'You don't see a government in charge,' said Peter Romero, the State Department's top official for Latin America, 'only plebiscites, referendums, more elections.'[17] The arrogance of the charges underlined the US Government's historic ignorance of Latin America's internal social and political processes. In a surprising endorsement of the Bolivarian constitution, a former Inter-American Human Rights Commission director described the new constitution as 'one of, if not the most advanced in the world in terms of human rights protection.'[18] Latinobarometro, a Santiago de Chile-based think tank which measures public attitudes toward democratic institutions, announced that Latin Americans had lost faith in democracy with the notable exception of Venezuela, where approval for the political system 'soared' from 35 per cent in 1998 to 55 per cent in the year 2000, a phenomenon pollsters directly attributed to the popularity of Hugo Chávez.[19]

The opposition demanded the postponement of the May 2000 elections after a pilot test of voting machinery resulted in chaos just days before the election. The poll was delayed by two months, despite opposition from Chávez, who was impatient to finish laying the foundations of his political project. When the elections finally went ahead on July 31st 2000, Chávez once more coasted to victory, winning a fresh presidential mandate with 59 per cent of the vote and a comfortable majority in the new assembly. The Bolivarian alliance won 15 of the 23 gubernatorial races while two more were occupied by sympathisers. President Chávez still lacked an organised political support base, however, relying on inexperienced outsiders and bandwagon jumpers keen to attach themselves to his ample coattails. Mayors, governors and councillors were elected simply by adding their names to the Chávez slate, spelling trouble ahead. The Chavista movement, still divided over the option of electoral participation, did not have sufficient activists to contest 6,000 posts around the country. In addition Chávez's coalition partners in the Patriotic Pole, notably the PPT, MAS and the Communist Party, grew impatient with the Venezuelan leader's strong leadership which denied them a distinct voice within the government. The Bolivarian revolution was still largely a one-man phenomenon observed by a large, cheering crowd in the background.

## The international situation

Meanwhile the 'Chávez factor' was felt beyond Venezuelan borders as a joint military-indigenous rebellion toppled the unpopular Ecuadorean president Jamil Mahuad in January 2000, making the army officer who led the military rebellion, a household name. 'I admire president Chávez's leadership and I will follow his example by entering the political arena,' said Lucio Gutiérrez, who was imprisoned for four months then released through an amnesty. In November 2002 the former colonel was elected President of Ecuador in a landslide vote,[20] while in Brazil Lula swept to power as the first democratically-elected socialist president in Latin America since Salvador Allende. Governments in Bolivia and Peru remained highly unstable while further south Argentina, once the IMF's star pupil, was unravelling at a furious pace and collapsed completely in December 2001. President Chávez's passionate attacks on the neo-liberal economic system, known in Latin America as the Washington Consensus, began to sound more and more like prophetic wisdom.

## 2001 – the year of enabling legislation

President Chávez now possessed the constitutional and legislative tools required to launch his 'peaceful, democratic revolution', but he lacked enabling legislation with which to implement his plans. A second Ley Habilitante gave Chávez the presidential power to approve a package of 49 laws which would enable the state to implement the promises enshrined in the new constitution. The 49 laws were formally approved in November 2001, marking the point of no return for Chávez's troubled relations with business, church and media leaders. Fedecamaras, Venezuela's powerful business lobby, bitterly opposed the new laws and set about actively undermining the Chávez administration. The Venezuelan Worker's Confederation, led by Carlos Ortega, rowed in alongside their traditional rivals, setting aside historic differences.

## The CTV

The Workers' Confederation of Venezuela, or CTV, was founded in 1936 and quickly established a reputation as a lobbyist not only for organised labour but for the poor majority. The organisation launched a successful oil strike in 1936–37, uniting the entire country against the 'oil imperialists', demanding greater revenues from the foreign oil companies that still controlled the industry. In 1950 the CTV participated in another popular strike, this time challenging the military government of Marcos Pérez Jiménez, while in 1980 the trade union movement surprised its own membership by demanding worker participation in decision-making processes at the workplace. During the Caracazo in February 1989 the CTV came down on the side of the street protestors in denouncing an IMF austerity package and called a general strike against President Carlos Andrés Pérez.

In the 1990s the CTV moderated its demands, accepted the neo-liberal privatisation agenda and gave up on the marginalised sectors once championed by its leaders. The union let pass the privatisation of the health sector which created a two-tiered health-care system and put up no resistance to labour reforms that cut redundancy payments. CTV membership and influence waned in direct proportion to the rise of the informal economy, leaving just 12 per cent of the workforce currently on its books. An opinion poll in the 1990s ranked the CTV tenth in a list of twelve institutions in descending order of popular trust. Even the notoriously inefficient police and the judicial system scored higher.[21] The reasons for the decline were the lack of popular consultation with the grassroots, the absence of agitation against the neo-liberal agenda, and the acceptance of labour reforms which rolled back historic labour gains. The CTV maintained close links to social democratic Acción Democrática and the catastrophic decline of that party in the 1990s also contributed to the CTV's downward trend.

When Chávez assumed office he declared war on the CTV, eliminating subsidies and threatening to dissolve the leadership structure. In April 1999 the CTV called its Fourth Extraordinary Congress, launching an internal democratisation process in an attempt to take the wind out of Chávez's sails. The CTV agreed to hold direct elections for the organisation's executive committee posts and sidelined discredited union leaders. Further reforms that had been consistently blocked prior to Chávez's election victory were quickly approved. In December 1999 Chávez won a mandate through referendum to reorganise the union sector, although abstention, which was now running at 77 per cent, critically undermined the legitimacy of the process. The Chávez trade union sector failed to take advantage of their leader's enormous popularity, undecided as to whether their role should be one of unconditional support for the Bolivarian project or that of creating an autonomous trade union sector. During the constituent assembly debates the four elected union delegates pursued demands for the reduction of the working week from 44 to 40 hours and a reduction in the night shift from 40 to 35 hours. One of the union delegates acknowledged that 'the main Chávez leaders in the assembly sometimes communicated party line to the delegates by a simple gesture, as in the case of the working week, but many delegates voted as they wished anyhow.'[22]

The Bolivarian workers' movement set its sights on the nation's informal sector, which encompasses over 50 per cent of the working population, and who have no formal representative body. The informal sector draws its workforce largely from the populous barrios where Chávez's support has its deepest roots, facilitating its incorporation into the government's development plans. The CTV blocked the incorporation of informal workers into the organisation despite the legal recognition granted by the Labour Ministry.

The election process for the CTV executive body was bitter. The absence of the informal vote played a part in the defeat of the Chávez candidate as Carlos Ortega, supported by Acción Democrática, won 57 per cent of the vote, leagues ahead of Chavista delegate Aristobulo Isturiz, who polled just 16 per cent of votes. The election, held in October 2001, paved the way for the general strike of April 2002. The reformed CTV union bureaucrats were back on their feet, mobilising among oil workers, teachers, steel workers and public employees. However the CTV had insufficient support to challenge Chávez alone and relied heavily on its traditional adversary, the employers' body Fedecamaras and its middle class support base, to attempt the brief coup in April 2002. The subsequent general strike launched in December 2002 was a failure as most workers rejected the CTV-Fedecamaras heave against Chávez, recognising the anti-labour sentiments at the heart of the conflict.

The Ley de Tierras proposed the legal recognition of the urban squatters who have for decades occupied vast tracts of land on the edges of large cities, building labyrinthine housing networks independent of state influence. The land law also prepared an 'agrarian revolution', which would distribute land to poor farmers, along with credits and technical advice. The law was vehemently opposed by the land-owning elite, who saw the move as the beginning of a Cuban-style break-up of large farms and expropriation of idle lands.

In the economic arena, a new hydrocarbon law opened up private investment opportunities in the oil industry, a significant shift which passed largely unnoticed as government and opposition alike focused on social provisions contained in the 49 laws. Chávez came in for criticism from his former mentor Douglas Bravo, who described the Bolivarian process as 'democratic neo-liberalism', the lesser of two evils, battling the 'fascist neo-liberalism' of Venezuela's traditional power brokers. The '49 laws' quickly came to represent the *plus ultra non* of the Venezuelan system, the point at which business, media, oil, church and other influential sectors threw down the gauntlet and demanded the government relent or face total resistance to its continued rule. After three years of debate, referenda and tightrope-walking, Chávez finally nailed his ideological sails to the mast, preparing for 2002, the 'year of revolutionary offensive'.

## Bolivarian circles

In June 2001, Chavista leaders called for the organisation of a support network to promote and defend the ideals of the Bolivarian project. President Chávez's government remained a moveable feast of army comrades, university professors and the occasional veteran politician, rotating posts with remarkable speed. By 2003 the post of Presidential Communication Chief, which achieved ministerial rank in 2001, had seen nine occupants. President Chávez always seemed to be in a rush to get somewhere, demanding more from his ministers, a revolving door syndrome that prompted improvisation and hasty decision-making. As Chávez's more radical enemies prepared to challenge his project it became clear that a solid organisational support base was required.

On December 17th 2001, at a rally attended by half a million people, President Chávez launched the Bolivarian Circles (*Círculos Bolivarianos*, CBs), neighbourhood organisations aimed at 'raising the consciousness of citizens, developing all forms of participatory organisation, stimulating creativity and innovation in the life of the individual and the community … and co-ordinating projects of interest to the community in the area of health, education, culture, sport, public services, housing, preservation of the environment, natural resources and our historical heritage.'

It is estimated that about 1.5 million people signed up to the Bolivarian Circles, nearly 10 per cent of the country's adult population. The only requirement of such circles was to register at a government building, which six months later was still inundated with community organisers seeking to formalise their groups into the vast Bolivarian network. Three officials worked all day in a cramped basement office beside the presidential palace where men and women of all ages turned up with dog-eared folders announcing local projects ranging from sewing circles to literacy classes. Many activists joined up out of conviction while others registered in the hope of receiving state funds for pre-existing community groups. One Bolivarian Circle was established with the modest goal of 'studying the Bolivarian constitution', as impoverished Petare residents studied all 350 articles to find out what benefits they might gain from the new document. No political affiliation was required but everyone involved was expected to swear loyalty to the Bolivarian constitution.

The opposition has repeatedly claimed that the Bolivarian Circles are organising armed militias to attack the middle classes. Venezuela is an armed society where two thirds of the population own a handgun and grenades and assault rifles are easily available on the black market. Logic dictates that citizens inclined to pro- or anti-Chávez positions will bring their private arsenals to bear on unfolding events. It seems safe to assume that if Chávez had an armed militia network it would have acted during the April 2002 coup attempt, bringing violence to the streets to resist the removal of their leader. The only organised armed group that claims any loyalty to Chávez is the Tupamaros, a Marxist-Leninist outfit which supports the Chávez administration but criticises the slow pace of the revolution, convinced that the moderate reformers have the upper hand in the process. Members of the Tupamaro group took to the streets during the April 2002 coup, engaging police in sporadic firefights, but never looking like a serious obstacle to the coup plotters.

The media has made much of the Bolivarian Liberation Forces (*Fuerzas Bolivarianas de Liberación*, FBL), a phantom rebel group charged with rural kidnappings and a terror campaign against opponents of the Chávez administration. There isn't a shred of evidence to sustain the claims beyond the accusations of celebrity journalists, who always manage to have a TV camera standing by when the *atentados* occur. The

FBL are proud of their affiliation, scattering leaflets that celebrate Hugo Chávez's intellectual responsibility in supporting terror attacks. In one case the media dedicated acres of space to the kidnapping of Sergio Omar Calderón, a former COPEI politician seized by gunmen at his country farm. The FBL was immediately blamed for the incident and even the US Government got in on the act, calling for Chávez to rein in the dogs of war. On the same day that Calderón was seized a Patria Para Todos (PPT) activist was assassinated. His death was reported without fanfare then immediately forgotten. Calderón was front-page news for the entire kidnap period, which lasted thirty days. When he was freed, Calderón immediately discounted any political motive to the kidnap, saying the kidnappers had Colombian accents and seemed indifferent to the Chávez regime. 'At times they treated him like a joke' said Calderón.

On the other hand, there is considerable evidence to suggest that middle- and upper-class citizens hostile to Chávez are organising through security networks in apartment blocks. In the aftermath of the Caracazo of February 1989 frightened citizens purchased weapons to protect themselves against the threat of renewed social unrest. A decade later the nation's middle and upper classes perceived a new threat to their security and privileges, this time the *hordas Chavistas*, the dispossessed majority seething in the hillsides around Caracas, empowered by the Bolivarian message of redemption.

Once the existence of the Bolivarian Circles was formally announced the opposition began to blame them for every incident of street violence. By 2003 the neighbourhood circles had been largely overshadowed by the *Círculos Patrióticos*, or Patriotic Circles, the Bolivarian movement's latest attempt to organise its supporters into an organic, card-carrying support base. Chávez's political project, subordinate at all times to his leadership, has yet to find an effective vehicle to convert its support into a party machine. The populist, caudillo-based appeal of Bolivarianismo, and its constant tug of war with the opposition, has created implacable obstacles in the way of establishing such a body.

Opposition to the 49 laws only hardened Chávez's resolve and inspired him to ever-greater rhetorical heights. In December 2001, Fedecamaras and the CTV launched a one-day general strike, protesting the new laws and the sacking of PDVSA executives who rejected government reforms to the oil company. The mobilisation attracted thousands of people, many of them drawn by the employers' federation promise of a day's salary if they took to the streets. The opposition warned the government that if the 49 laws were not amended they would return to the streets and force the government into retreat. The stage was now set for a dramatic showdown in early 2002.

## Chávez on the world stage

Like all rebels looking for a path, Chávez cast a wide net in search of ideological inspiration. Shortly after he was released from prison in 1994 he made contact with Norberto Ceresole, a right-wing Argentinian nationalist whose ideas had a strong impact on the Venezuelan leader. Ceresole was a sociologist and advisor to Argentina's *Carapintada* movement, which had tried to topple President Raúl Alfonsín when he attempted to bring army leaders to account for crimes against humanity.[23]

Ceresole viewed the seizing of state power as a matter of uniting three poles: caudillo-army-people. The caudillo would transform the military into the armed wing of a nationalist revolutionary project and enlist the poor as its popular support base. Ceresole predicted that the leader of such a political project would provoke a strategic confrontation between a unipolar and multipolar world, in which the caudillo would face down the global hegemony of the US by rallying all factors hostile to US power. A multipolar axis would emerge, involving left-wing guerrillas, progressive social movements and non-aligned governments in Europe, Latin America and the Middle East. Ceresole described his ideas as 'post-democratic', as the caudillo would sweep aside parliament, courts and other institutions which slowed down decision-making processes and reined in ambitious presidential projects.

Chávez also visited Colombia in 1994, invited by former M-19 guerrilla leaders, where he called for the revival of the Bolivarian Anfictrionic Congresses, a series of meetings in which Bolívar attempted to build a 'Greater Colombia' stretching from Panama to Argentina. Chávez met Cuban leader Fidel Castro the same year; what began as a strategic relationship would blossom into a lasting friendship. However, the transition from army rebel to national statesman required a complete revision of Chávez's strategic political project. When the Venezuelan media kicked up a fuss about the presence of Ceresole, the disgruntled right-wing ideologue was unceremoniously booted out of the country. Chávez had a habit of picking up allies along the way as he needed them then discarding them as soon as political pragmatism required; Douglas Bravo had suffered the same fate.

On the global stage Venezuela's oil industry would act as a platform for an OPEC revival, a fundamental pillar of a multipolar world. When Hugo Chávez assumed office, oil prices stood at just US$9 a barrel, a figure which rose to $33 within eighteen months, providing a remarkable boost to state revenues. Chávez played a key role in revitalising OPEC, the moribund organisation of petroleum exporting countries. In March 1999, Oil Minister Ali Rodríguez announced that Venezuela would respect agreed production cutbacks, marking a historic turnaround from the nation's traditional pro-US oil policy. Rodríguez, a former guerrilla who fought alongside Douglas Bravo in the 1960s, had been the oil expert for La Causa R and PPT, two parties which backed Chávez's bid for presidential power. Closer to home, Chávez proposed the Confederation of Latin American States and signed a memorandum of agreement with Brazilian president Fernando Henrique Cardoso to create Petroamerica, describing it as an 'enormous energy integration plan, born in Venezuela's Orinoco river, flowing down the Amazon and along our fluvial passages to emerge in Río de la Plata in Argentina.' Unlike traditional caudillos, however, Chávez's alternative political project was endorsed time and again at the polls.

President Chávez took his vision to the world, assuming the presidency of the Group of 77 developing countries at the United Nations in the first week of January 2001. He argued the case for a 'multipolar' world in which the existence of more than one world power would guard against the emergence of an omnipotent global bully. Latin America has traditionally been subservient to US foreign policy goals with Cuba in particular suffering the tightest embargo in the world, an armed invasion and the permanent threat of aggression. The subsequent behaviour of the administration under George W. Bush in prosecuting an illegal war against Iraq highlighted Chávez's counsel, but individual countries remain prey to US economic and political pressure.

The Chávez administration voted against US-sponsored resolutions in the international arena, blocking censure of China, Cuba and Iran for human rights violations. The president also turned down US requests to fly drug interception missions in Venezuelan airspace as well as US offers to send the Army Corps of Engineers following the devastating floods in Vargas state in December 1999.[24] In sharp contrast, Chávez embraced Cuban leader Fidel Castro and declared that the people of both nations were 'swimming in the same sea of happiness' – a particularly offensive statement given the extraordinary and often lethal lengths to which Cubans resort in order to leave the island. Chávez established a Cuba– Venezuela co-operation programme that has imported Cuban health and literacy initiatives along with techniques for urban agriculture. Each programme has received international recognition for its merits, but Chávez has unnecessarily stirred up trouble by highlighting the growing Cuban presence in Venezuela at every opportunity. Even Chávez's own supporters have their doubts about the Castro regime. The official organ of the Coordinadora Simón Bolívar, *Al Son del 23* (January 2002 issue) made the following comment on dictatorship, which could well be taken as a criticism of the Cuban system: 'the person who eats but does not have the right to free speech is as unhappy as the person who has the right to speak out but has nothing to eat.' Chávez himself is not above poking fun at the Cuban regime, on one occasion exchanging good-natured banter with *Prensa Latina*'s Caracas-based correspondent, gently mocking Castro's 'miraculous' election results.[25]

The opposition made much of Chávez's decision to sell oil at preferential prices to Cuba, but he afforded the same privilege to fifteen poor nations in Central America and the Caribbean. In a similar vein, Chávez has made official visits to Spain, France and the US that draw no hostile commentary. In contrast, his brief oil-industry related stopovers in Libya, Iraq and Iran (he was in Iraq for all of twelve hours) were blown out of proportion, given the vital national business interests at play there.

## Utopian dreams:
## rural resettlement and urban markets

While Chávez sculpted the required constitutional and legislative tools he also took steps to begin immediate welfare provision to the poor. Chávez's pilot army-civic co-operation project, Plan Bolívar 2000, was launched on February 27th 1999, the tenth anniversary of the Caracazo, when army troops were dispatched to quell civil unrest. This time army troops were sent to repair roads and build health clinics, a symbolic operation to mend army–civilian relations and demonstrate the efficiency of the armed forces in delivering social benefits.

Unemployed and indigent citizens were given small payments to work alongside the soldiers, establishing a pattern whereby marginalised urban men, easy prey for drugs and crime, would join the Bolivarian network in return for financial reward. This policy has fuelled criticism of Chávez for engaging in populist tactics to build grassroots loyalty to the government. Plan Bolívar 2000 also established a food distribution network as troops would load cheese, meat and fruit onto their trucks and set up improvised stalls in public plazas, where they sold their goods at the lowest available prices. The local shopkeepers were less than impressed: 'They're damaging our livelihood and hurting our image,' said one butcher in a working-class Caracas neighbourhood. 'We're not speculators, we're just trying to make a living and of course the army, with all its resources can sell products at prices cheaper than ours.'[26] The army-run stalls still exist but by 2003 the new 'Bolivarian Markets' had largely replaced them as neighbourhood committees organise local weekend markets along similar lines. In Petare, one of the largest working-class districts in Caracas, a local activist explained to me how the market was run: 'Each Wednesday we meet the market stallholders and fix prices for the following weekend,' she said. The prices were established after an exhaustive check on the cost of foodstuffs. 'We offer the stallholder a prime spot right in the heart of the neighbourhood in return for agreeing to abide by the fair price system.' In addition each stallholder had to pay a $1 fee to set up the stall, with the proceeds going toward a community project.[27]

Plan Bolívar 2000 performed an important task, but it closely resembled the 'assistentialist' programmes favoured by the traditional political parties and in a similar vein was hampered by allegations of corruption. Millions of dollars were allegedly siphoned away to non-existent companies for services which were never delivered to the social development scheme.[28]

## SARAO

It was clear by this point that President Chávez had no master plan for governing the country, other than a passionate vision of an economic system that would deliver a new deal to the majority poor. Once in office Chávez and his cabinet studied hundreds of projects aimed at reducing poverty and easing urban overcrowding. 'Bring me solutions, not problems,' was a favourite presidential catchphrase. Planning Minister Jorge Giordani hired alternative architect Enrique Vila, a town planner with a keen eye for sustainable rural housing. Vila worked on a national housing survey which evaluated the state of every home in rural Venezuela in 1973, then wrote up a 65-page dossier which mapped out a vision of a new integral rural development scheme. President Chávez read the blueprint and gave the project his enthusiastic backing. If successful, Vila's plan will transform the nation's poor farmers into prosperous middle-class citizens, dovetailing perfectly with a parallel plan to reclaim urban areas for agricultural production. The plan also linked in to Chávez's regional focus on food security, a concern shared by governments in Brazil and Argentina. The UN human settlement programme, UN-Habitat, based in Nairobi, issued a report in October 2003 in which it was calculated that every third person in the world will be a shantytown resident within 30 years. The authors of the report found that the rural–urban exodus was prompted by the privatisation of public services and job losses in agriculture, concluding that 'cities have become a dumping ground for people working in unskilled, unprotected and low-wage industries and trades.'[29]

The Venezuelan project aimed at revitalising the countryside was named SARAO, *Sistema de Asociaciones Rurales Auto-Organizadas*, or System of Self-organised Rural Associations. (The word formed by the acronym also means 'party'.) In simple terms it is a network of interrelated co-operatives. Each SARAO is a farming unit involving twelve families in a 'circular metabolism' that combines food crops, waste management, appropriate technology and autonomous organisation to achieve a high degree of self-reliance. Each family grows four different crops, insuring a broad diet and surplus crops for resale. The community has a meeting hall, school system and a connection to the outside world through rail, boat or road transport. Leaving Caracas one can see rural railway stations undergoing refurbishment while two major bridges are in construction to connect urban and rural population centres. The SARAOs plan to develop a LETTS-type scheme in which communities pool resources and exchange goods and services using an alternative currency to encourage the accumulation of social capital. Each SARAO unit has approximately 24 adults plus children, and twelve units are regarded as the ideal figure to maximise resources, giving a potential SARAO population cluster a thousand inhabitants. Each SARAO network will be linked to the country's agronomy institutes, providing a steady supply of student volunteers who will spend time working there as part of their course assessment.

I visited the pilot SARAO community of El Chaguaramal, which appears on no map and cannot be found without the help of a willing local. I was told to look out for a man with a large paunch and a hairpin moustache at a sleazy truck stop along the Panamerican highway two hours east of Caracas. I wasn't disappointed. Roberto welcomed me aboard his ancient Dodge pickup, pausing long enough to ogle some passing women, then drove several miles along a dirt track that led to a colourful, circular housing project set amidst fields of crops. El Chaguaramal is located in Venezuela's tropical lowlands, where sunset is greeted with deep drumming by the descendants of former black slaves. SARAO members lined up to chat about their new lives, displaying real excitement at the tasks ahead. In order to qualify for the project, members must be unemployed or on a low salary, own no land and have at least one child. Women are equal partners in the home and in the field – a tough pill for most men to swallow in this *Machista* society.

## Guerrilla gardeners feed the Hilton Hotel

Back in Caracas I was curious to witness the parallel 'rural-isation' of urban life. The pilot urban garden project is a vegetable patch down by the Hilton Hotel, on one side of a busy bridge linking a six-lane city highway. Lettuces and tomatoes sprout incongruously in a converted park area as vehicles whizz by and street traders sell their wares. A dozen workers wash and clean vegetables while others explain to curious passersby what's going on. 'When we first started people stopped to laugh at us,' explained Rafael, a former oil worker. 'Now when they come by and see the lettuces and tomatoes for sale they ask us when they can have their own plot out in the suburbs.' The city centre garden produces a range of vegetables and medicinal plants sold at below average prices. The co-op members include an unemployed cobbler, chemist, accountant, plumber, teacher and tourist guide, with one thing in common: zero experience of agriculture. 'We are all children or grand-children of farmers who came to Caracas in search of jobs,' said Rafael. 'It didn't take long to catch on.' It's a remarkable sight to behold a strategic plot of land in the heart of Caracas where property valued at $1,000 per square metre is producing lettuces sold at 25 cents each. 'This is a tool to help change the attitude of ordinary Venezuelans,' explained Angelina. 'You can't put a monetary value on community,' she said, adding, 'garden plots bring people together.' The scale is impressive, with an area of just 3,800 square metres capable of producing seven tonnes of vegetables a month. When classes restart in September 2003, school groups will begin daily visits designed to inspire similar projects in schoolyards throughout the city. The government has already begun similar food plots in hospitals, army barracks and prisons, giving inmates a chance to improve their diet. I wondered if government loyalty was a prerequisite for joining the co-op but Rafael balked at the notion. 'I have my own way of thinking,' he said, 'no one ever asked me whether I voted for Chávez or not.'

In addition to the rural suburbs and urban vegetable fields, Chávez's bureaucrats are mapping out a vast swathe of idle territory, an estimated three million hectares of fertile land located beneath the main population belt on the northern Venezuelan coast. The ambitious rural resettlement and national food security projects were scoffed at by journalists and politicians, who offered unkind parallels with Soviet gulags. How on earth could an urban family survive in hostile climatic conditions far from their usual sources of entertainment and employment? Nature answered the question in December 1999 when sudden rainfalls buried makeshift neighbourhoods, killing at least 30,000 people. On a visit to inspect the damage caused by the mudslides, citizens repeatedly asked me how they could apply for the resettlement scheme which was still at the drawing board stage. 'Anywhere but here' they said, fearful that sudden rains, ominous symptoms of global climate change, would return to swallow thousands more people living in precarious conditions on the edge of the city.

The SARAO at El Chaguaramal is the first of its kind; experiments are also taking place in Zulia and Tachira states, where different climates and terrain demand different approaches. The SARAO will not show any significant returns for another ten years as land is mapped out, volunteers canvassed and Venezuelans groomed for a major change in their lifestyles. Resettled families require housing grants, farming credits and technical assistance, along with government food programmes that guarantee fair prices for agricultural produce. Although anyone signing up to the SARAO is taking a huge gamble on an uncertain future – what happens if the next government decides that the entire project is a waste of time and money and consigns it to the rubbish bin?

The co-op members receive joint titles to their land, but no property titles are issued for the homes which belong to the SARAO families only for as long as they participate in the co-operative. 'None of us are brothers here but as the project has been getting on its feet we have got to know each other and now we consider each other brothers,' said Joaquín Cabrera, a former employee on a nearby cocoa plantation. The cost of the project is relatively low as the state targets idle or state-owned land. The Chaguaramal project was established on army land donated for the purpose. The houses are simple constructions with high roofs and cool porches while an electricity sub-station supplies low-cost energy. Each family takes on a small loan that is repaid in five years, a sum far lower than the cheapest rents in Caracas. The SARAO members are aware of the significance of this pilot scheme: 'This is the first government that ever paid attention to the poor,' said Douglas Petrizzo, 'I want this to work and multiply across the country.'

## Taking stock

As the first three years of the Chávez administration drew to a close in December 2001, supporters and detractors rushed to pass judgement. The opposition pointed to high crime figures, stagnant poverty rates and the growing climate of confrontation on the streets. Defenders of the Bolivarian project boasted a drop in unemployment, the cancellation of school fees that allowed 600,000 more children to enter the education system, improvement in child nutrition rates, a reduction in infant mortality, the provision of 10,000 microcredits by the Banco del Pueblo since October 1999 and 6,286 small projects authorised for women by the Banco de las Mujeres. In the Amazon 19 indigenous peoples threw their weight behind the Chávez reforms which facilitated the election of a regional representative to the new legislative assembly while an indigenous delegate became state governor for the Amazon. 'The year 2002 will be dedicated to improving health and delivering safe water,' said Bernabé Arana, indigenous mayor of Autama, an Amazon village.

Land ownership remained savagely uneven, with one per cent of owners controlling 60 per cent of productive lands. But the new land reform law, one of the controversial package of 49 laws, promised to 'eliminate' the *latifundios* (large estates), described as 'a system that contravenes justice and the general interest and social peace in the countryside.'

The development of the agricultural sector was defined as 'the fundamental means of attending, in an efficient and effective way, to the population's food requirements.' Meanwhile the new Fishing Law would extend Venezuela's protected coastal fishing area from three to six miles, an important advantage for local fishermen.

The ambitious development plan was finally at the starting blocks as Chávez prepared to demonstrate that his Bolivarian project could deliver social welfare and economic growth.

## Notes

1  Hugo Chávez, speech given at the World Social Forum, Porto Alegre, Brazil, January 2003.
2  *The Tablet*, October 9, 1999.
3  *The Financial Times*, May 12, 1999.
4  *The Economist*, July 31, 1999.
5  *El País*, August 25, 1999.
6  Buxton, J. 2001, *The Failure of Political Reform in Venezuela*, Aldershot: Ashgate, p33.
7  *The Financial Times*, August 1999.
8  *El Financiero*, November 29, 1999.
9  *El País*, August 24, 1999.
10  Ellner, S., Hellinger, D. 2003, *La Política Venezolana en la época de Chávez*, Caracas: Nueva Sociedad, p129.
11  El País November 23, 1999.
12  Ellner, pp238–9.
13  'Venezuelan Potentate', *The New York Times*, August 23, 1999.
14  *The News*, December 1st, 1999.
15  *El Nacional*, December 19, 1999.
16  *El Universal*, July 11, 2003.
17  *The Economist*, February 5, 2000.

18  *El Universal*, December 13, 1999.

19  *The Financial Times*, May 11, 2000.

20  *El Nacional*, June 4, 2000.

21  Ellner, p214.

22  Froilan Barrios, president of the Frente Constituyente de Trabajadores/
    FCT, August 1, 2001, quoted in Ellner, p225.

23  Ceresole died in May 2003.

24  Ellner, p18.

25  El día del periodista, June 27, 2002.

26  *The New York Times*, April 13, 1999.

27  Personal Interview, July 2002.

28  Ellner, p137.

29  The *Guardian*, October 4, 2003.

# 3
## Reaction

"You tell me who's going to get this country going, a layabout who spends the day drinking rum or someone like me with a post-graduate degree in the United States?"

Marisela Pinedo, chemical engineer, aged 27.

The Venezuelan opposition organised a huge demonstration for January 23rd 2002 while Chávez led a counter-demonstration the same day as both sides measured street support in advance of a more serious showdown. The tension rose several notches when media reports hinted at mutiny inside the army barracks if Chávez failed to 'rectify' his economic policies. The US Government joined the chorus, loudly criticising the Chávez administration for its lack of enthusiasm in supporting the so-called war on terror.

On February 18th 2002 the Bolívar fell 5.5 per cent against the dollar while a senior navy officer, Rear-Admiral Carlos Molina, who was also ambassador-designate to Greece, resigned his post and called on Chávez to leave office. Molina criticised Chávez for 'repeatedly violating the constitution … and for abusing the national assembly and supreme court.' In addition, US Government officials issued three thinly veiled warnings against Chávez that week; CIA director George Tenet told the US Senate Intelligence Committee that he was 'particularly worried about Venezuela, our third oil supplier.' The *Washington Post* published an article citing a State Department official who warned that Venezuela was in 'a precarious and dangerous position' and that if Chávez didn't 'fix things soon' then he 'would not finish his period in office.' Colin Powell warned the US Senate that he doubted if 'Chávez really believes in democracy', citing as evidence the Venezuelan leader's visits to Iraq and Libya.

Venezuelan coup plotters visited the White House around this time, gauging support for their upcoming adventure. US officials said nothing that might cause them to change their plans. On March 5th CTV leader Carlos Ortega signed a 'governability pact' with employers' union Fedecamaras, with the Catholic Church serving as witness to the demand for 'the democratic and constitutional exit' of the government. The gloves were off. The media echoed the growing call for a heave against Chávez. In response, a group of about one hundred Chavistas protested noisily outside the offices of *El Nacional*. The event recalled the Argentinian *escraches*, where citizens protested outside the homes of agents of repression and their collaborators, naming and shaming the torturers in the absence of legal mechanisms for bringing them to justice. There was some pushing and shoving of journalists by both sides during the street rallies despite the efforts of some journalists who vainly attempted to explain the difference between a news reporter on the street and a media executive in the clubhouse.

In a newspaper supplement titled 'War Correspondents?' Venezuelan journalists examined the deteriorating situation. Felix Gerardi, a photographer with *El Universal*, recalled how he was beaten up while attending an anti-Chávez demonstration. 'The crowd were taking a camera from someone so I took a photo of what was happening,' explained Gerardi, 'but the crowd thought I was with the other person and turned on me.' Gerardi was surprised to observe a Metropolitan Police patrol watching the fracas but doing nothing to aid the reporters.[1] The situation descended into farce as reporters working for corporate media outlets went about their business wearing bulletproof vests and gas masks, accompanied by a police escort of up to four officers. 'It's an uncomfortable situation,' said Globovision reporter Johnny Ficarella. 'We're not responsible for what's happening.' These comments conveniently ignored the fact that reporters were working for media bosses who had launched a blatant campaign of incitement to hatred against Chávez. By the time the oil strike began in December 2002, media analysts logged 700 pro-strike advertisements on television each day while normal programming was replaced with advertisements sponsored by the oil industry billed as 'public service announcements'. [2]

President Chávez ignored US Government criticism and derided the sporadic military defections as isolated acts of desperation. The year 2001, insisted Chávez, would be the year of the consolidation of the revolution. But the deteriorating economic situation affected huge swathes of the population as inflation and speculation drove up basic food prices. Chávez called on members of the Bolivarian Circles to inform the government of 'excessive' price rises on non-imported goods: 'I call on the Bolivarian Circles to wage war on the speculators,' said Chávez, who added, with characteristic bombast, 'go to the supermarkets and warehouses and call the vice-president.' This call to arms was vintage Chávez populism, combining an appeal to citizen participation with a sense of government commitment to each citizen, with the vice-president waiting at the end of a phone to hear every individual complaint.

The management sector at the oil company PDVSA also showed its disapproval of Chávez's evolving project as several executives resigned or were sacked due to their opposition to the restructuring of the company. Business leaders, military dissidents, the private media, church leaders and displaced politicians were now actively plotting the overthrow of the government, combining street mobilisation with cash offers estimated at $100,000 to high-ranking army officers should they agree to jump ship and denounce Chávez. Every time

Chávez appeared on television a round of pot-banging would ring out in middle-class Venezuelan apartments as the struggle for control of Venezuela was played out home by home, apartment block by apartment block. Fedecamaras organised several mobilisations, paying their workers to take the day off, an ironic turn of events in a region where such federations are more likely to hire gunmen to get rid of troublesome strikers. The opposition turned up the heat on the government, counting on Chávez to cave in to avoid possible bloodshed. In an interview with this reporter which took place shortly before the April 2002 coup, the Venezuelan leader outlined the strength of his radical social project: 'It has all been peacefully achieved without a single stain to blot the democratic process, with full respect for freedom of expression and human rights.'

Chávez's evident pride in his achievement was understandable, especially in the context of a region where state terror is a routine instrument of government policy. Neighbouring Colombia is the most dangerous country in the world in which to be a trade unionist; the International Federation of Free Trade Unions (ICFTU) reported that of 213 union victims in 2002, 184 were killed in Colombia. Journalists and lawyers suffer the same fate in Mexico, army troops murder coca farmers protesting peacefully in the Bolivian jungles, and Argentinian police murder picketing strikers with impunity. In July 2002, democratically-elected Peruvian president Alejandro Toledo declared martial law and sent tanks into the city of Arequipa to quell anti-privatisation protests, while a Peruvian journalist was beaten to death by state-backed killers.

President Chávez relied on his traditional bluster to frighten off opposition elements. In his weekly television show, "Aló Presidente", broadcast on the state-run Channel 8, he offered this advice to his enemies: 'I know how many of you are out there and I even know what you weigh after you've eaten breakfast.' (The programme began at the same time each week but one never knew what time it would come to an end. On the occasion of his 100th Aló Presidente, Chávez's loquacity ran to six hours and 34 minutes.) The military and business coup plotters had assembled the various jigsaw pieces but lacked one vital element: bloodshed. No matter how aggressively and disrespectfully Chávez behaved, he was, if anything hyper-democratic, permitting a level of free speech that bordered on recklessness as the private media urged army officers and citizens to disown the democratically-elected government of the day.

## The coup

The business and trade union leadership called a general strike for April 9th and 10th in defence of PDVSA, which was undergoing extensive reform. The Chávez administration asserted its right to appoint management which would implement government policy rather than sabotage it. Several executives were sacked and a dozen more 'retired'.

On April 11 the employer and union federations declared the strike 'indefinite' and ordered Chávez to resign or face the consequences. A crowd of approximately 200,000 people converged on the offices of PDVSA that morning, where Fedecamaras leader Carlos Ortega suddenly urged the crowd to go to the presidential palace at Miraflores. 'With a great sense of responsibility I address our nation to request in the name of democratic Venezuela. I do not rule out the possibility that this crowd, this human river marches united to Miraflores to expel a traitor of the Venezuelan people.' The crowd needed no further encouragement to march, setting the scene for a violent confrontation. What the vast majority of people on the march did not know was that the showdown outside the Miraflores Palace had already been planned – down to the last corpse.

Otto Neustadt, a CNN correspondent in Venezuela, received a phone call from an opposition activist the night before the march to PDVSA headquarters: 'The march will head to

Miraflores,' Neustadt was told, 'there will be killings and twenty high-ranking military officers will speak out against Chávez and demand his resignation.' On the very morning of the march Neustadt was one of a small group of journalists invited to record an announcement by Vice-Admiral Ramirez Pérez, an announcement that would not be made public until later that day. It read as follows: 'The President of the Republic has betrayed the trust of the people, he is massacring innocent people with snipers. Just now six people were killed and dozens wounded in Caracas.' Neustadt took up the story; 'I was with these men who were going to issue a communiqué against Chávez. I was there at least two hours before the killing started.'[3]

Opposition mobilisations had become a regular feature of the Caracas city centre landscape since December 2001. The vast majority of protestors came with peaceful intent, and protests had so far been contained with minimal violence – fisticuffs, stones and tear gas rather than fatalities. On the streets, news spread quickly that a hostile crowd was converging on the presidential palace. Thousands of Chávez supporters downed tools and converged on the city centre. The trap had been set.

The opposition reached the downtown area, approaching the presidential palace, where government followers gathered to prevent the storming of the building – the suspected goal of the opposition leaders. Two hundred metres from the building a group of National Guard troops vainly tried to hold back the anti-Chávez crowds while Metropolitan Police, under the orders of anti-Chávez mayor Alfredo Peña, parked their vehicles underneath a key bridge, Puente Llaguno, cutting off the Chavistas' access to the Miraflores building. At this point a distance of some two hundred metres separated the two factions.

The shooting began at about 2.30pm. The city streets turned into a deadly target range as snipers posted on rooftops using silencers shot into the crowds. The first four sniper victims were among the pro-Chávez supporters: 'I thought people had fainted or slipped and hurt themselves,' said Judith Galarza, an eyewitness to the chaotic events. But when pools of blood trickled from underneath the bodies panic ensued. Armed protestors on the Puente Llaguno bridge responded to Metropolitan Police fire while presidential guards tried to reach the rooftops where the snipers took aim at random targets. The local media immediately blamed the deaths on the president and demanded his resignation. The news spread quickly around the world: Chávez had spilled the blood of innocents, his administration had placed itself beyond the pale of civilised rule. The Bolivarian project had betrayed its origins in what seemed to be a re-run of the Caracazo, with unarmed citizens being killed to defuse an outburst of social tension.

The Venezuelan Army, cut off from events on the street but sworn never to turn its weapons against its own people, briefly hesitated. Chávez remained inside the presidential palace, surrounded by loyal guards. He needed to re-establish his authority and explain what had happened. As the killings began, Chávez addressed the nation on television. He spoke for over two hours, appealing for calm. The army gave TV stations the go-ahead to split their screens, broadcasting the president's words alongside images of the chaos unfolding just outside his office. Later that evening, when the full impact of the afternoon's events had begun to sink in, Chávez began a second televised address on state television, but the signal was quickly cut off. An anti-Chávez mob attacked Channel 8, the only station broadcasting interviews with Chávez officials. Meanwhile behind the scenes Venezuela's business and top figures in the Catholic Church hierarchy negotiated a transition government, counting on US and Spanish support.

Chávez remained in the palace after the killings, trying to get Channel 8 back onto the air in order to deliver a message to the nation, and it is unclear how much access to information he had about what was happening with the army at this time.

Surrounded by his closest advisors, Chávez weighed up his options. A phone call from the dissident army leaders cut short the discussion as renegade troops threatened to bomb Miraflores palace if Chávez didn't resign his post. At four in the morning members of the army high command entered Miraflores and demanded to take Chávez with them. General Lucas Rincón read the official communiqué: 'We have requested the resignation of the president. He has accepted.' The devastating message, an outright fabrication, was transmitted on television every 20 minutes throughout the following 36 hours. 'Venezuela has been liberated' was the repeated onscreen message displayed by TV stations as citizens stayed inside, fearful of looting and unrest.

Chávez was detained at an offshore military base, La Orchila, facing criminal charges for his responsibility in the deaths of civilians during the opposition march. He later said that he went quietly to avoid bloodshed, knowing that a word from him would be enough to ignite a civil war that could cost thousands of lives. But he never resigned.

Pedro Carmona, head of Fedecamaras, which had called the mobilisation that day, held a meeting with the army leadership at 7pm that evening, appointed himself interim president and set about organising a cabinet of like-minded business colleagues. In interviews after the coup Carmona would portray himself as an innocent victim of political intrigue who stepped reluctantly into the limelight to fill a political vacuum. The truth eventually emerged but was never given wide circulation in Venezuela. In fact, Carmona travelled to Spain in the days before the coup, where, among other things, he ordered a tailor to make him a presidential sash. (The sash returned with him when he cut short his attendance at a Madrid business conference to assume a leadership role in the planned coup attempt and was left behind in the rush to evacuate the presidential palace on the night of April 12th. It would form part of the material evidence implicating Carmona in the coup.) It also emerged that the powerful business leader had met with unnamed 'high-ranking' officials of the José María Aznar administration while in Spain, and that Prime Minister Aznar phoned Carmona and congratulated him on assuming office on April 12th.

Before Carmona travelled to Spain he also paid a visit to former president Carlos Andrés Pérez in the Dominican Republic, where CTV union leader Carlos Ortega was also in attendance, his travel costs funded by the conservative US group the National Endowment for Democracy. The CIA-funded Republican Institute also paid for opposition delegations to visit Washington DC and deliver dramatic horror stories outlining the 'Cubanisation' of Venezuela and the alleged slide toward authoritarian dictatorship.

The military–business coup was judged to have gone off perfectly, with far less victims than the average number of dead during a weekend of crime-fuelled killings in Caracas. In the shantytowns that ring Caracas's hillsides, however, no one believed the official story, relayed by the same media which had demonised Chávez and called for his ousting in the previous weeks and months. 'We want to see him, let him speak,' shouted one angry citizen to a passing foreign journalist. After two years of exaggeration, lies and distortion, it seemed Venezuela's partisan media networks had gone too far in their attempts to fabricate reality.

Pedro Carmona and his followers occupied Miraflores, naming a transition government that cheered gleefully when the new Attorney General announced the dissolution of congress, the annulment of the constitution, the sacking of governors and mayors and the axing of the ombudsman. The new junta announced the end of oil exports to Cuba and declared Colombian guerrillas 'narco-terrorists' in line with US foreign policy rhetoric.

During the Chávez administration there had been no political assassinations, no political prisoners and no media censorship, but the Carmona regime immediately launched an aggressive witch-hunt against Chávez officials while the Metropolitan

Police fired on Chávez supporters who took to the streets. 'If you know the whereabouts of Chavistas denounce them!' urged TV presenter Napoleón Bravo.[4] Over one hundred government sympathisers were imprisoned. A mob surrounded the Cuban embassy, destroying vehicles and cutting off water supplies, determined to force those inside to leave the building, and government officials and supporters went into hiding. The US Government welcomed the overthrow of Chávez, blaming the ousted president for provoking the crisis while looking forward to working to 'restore the essential elements of democracy.' A Bush administration official added that 'democratic legitimacy is more than a simple majority of votes' – a tidy if unconscious commentary on his own unelected boss George W. Bush. The European Union, under the presidency of Spain, joined the chorus of approval for the coup, along with ambassadors from Colombia and Chile.

## Radio Bemba

When it was clear that no message to the people from the media-savvy Chávez would be broadcast, 'Radio Bemba', the word-of-mouth network that carries rumour, gossip, suggestion and hard news like a powerful breeze through Latin America's populous barrios, suddenly sprang into action. The message carried on the wind was that Chávez never resigned, and the dead and injured outside Miraflores were mostly Chávez supporters. The next day Chavistas began to gather in small groups and descended from the hillsides to besiege the presidential palace demanding their leader's safe return. On April 13th the Carmona administration continued to swear in officials on behalf of the new regime, but at the same time the presidential guard, loyal to Chávez, quietly took control of Miraflores, using underground tunnels and prearranged signals.

The growing clamour of the angry crowds unnerved the 'transition government', sending generals, bishops and businesspeople scuttling to their cars to beat a path to the safety of their homes. In the late hours of Saturday April 13th members of Chávez's cabinet who had been in hiding regrouped inside the palace and began calling army barracks around the country. They quickly discovered that the military remained loyal to Chávez. As the tide turned and the pro-Chávez forces co-ordinated their leaders' return a news blackout was imposed by the corporate media. Venezuela's daily mass circulation newspapers voluntarily withdrew publication on April 14th with one paper, *El Nacional*, withdrawing a printed supplement celebrating the coup.

It was time to rescue Chávez. At the Maracay army barracks, just outside Caracas, General Raúl 'El Tao' Baduel swung into action: 'The philosophical aspect of the rescue plan was based on the Tao Te Ching,' Baduel later explained, thumbing through a copy of Lao Tse's classic text on warfare. 'There is no greater error than that of underestimating your enemy,' he read, before adding 'and the people behind the coup underestimated the Venezuelan people, viewing them as their enemies.' Baduel concluded that the motive of the coup plotters was 'greed and personal ambition for personal things or for power.' When two rival armies meet in such conditions, 'the side which comes with a painful heart will triumph.'

Just 47 hours after his tearful farewell, a helicopter returned Hugo Chávez to Miraflores palace. President Chávez was giddy and emotional but cautious too, thanking his supporters but requesting they return to their homes. He also pledged to 'sheathe' his sword, an acknowledgement that his own behaviour played a role in precipitating the events of the previous week. Carmona meanwhile was placed under house arrest pending an investigation, but fled to the Colombian embassy and then to the US.

An estimated 110 army officers were questioned on their role in the failed coup, with leading dissidents blaming Chávez's constitutional amendments for prodding them into action. Two generals and two admirals were absolved from

responsibility in events when the Supreme Court announced
that what happened on April 11th – known as 11-A – constituted
a 'power vacuum' rather than a coup d'etat, putting an end to
prosecution efforts. Analysts regarded the court decision as the
legitimisation of future coups while the *Financial Times*,
reporting from the 23 de Enero barrio, noted that 'a feeling of
anger is palpable among its 300,000 residents.'[5] The opposition, which had based its condemnation of Chávez on his
apparent efforts to create loyal institutions packed with militant
allies, now saw an opportunity to pursue lawsuits which might
result in the president's impeachment. Opposition lawyers
lodged 61 cases against the president, denouncing Chávez for,
among other things, signing an oil pact with Cuba, distorting
the role of the armed forces and even for alleged insanity.

The court decision to absolve the coup plotters was greeted
with violent clashes and fifteen people were shot and injured as
police fired on Chávez supporters who had besieged the court
building.[6] Chávez reacted by retiring some army commanders
while promoting others who had remained loyal to him during
the April crisis. The failure to clamp down on active army dissidents emboldened them to strike again within six months, but
by then the army hierarchy was committed to acting within
constitutional guidelines: 'If an army officer declares himself in
public it means he doesn't have the support of the army,'
concluded Francisco Ameliach, president of the Parliamentary
Defence Commission. Ameliach was in a good position to gauge
the issue, as he had participated in the February 1992 military
adventure. He insisted that conspiracies of any relevance take
place in silence and are only revealed to the wider public when
the day of action has arrived. The US military was unmasked as
a key player in the coup, with Lt Col James Rodger and Colonel
Ronald McCammon advising the coup plotters from their base
on the fifth floor of the Venezuelan army command centre,
although the US State Department denied playing any part in
the coup.[7]

Pedro Carmona was the public face of the coup, but it emerged that there were more strings pulled behind the scenes by a fishing partner of George Bush Senior. Gustavo Cisneros is one of Latin America's wealthiest and most influential individuals and a virulent opponent of Chávez. Cisneros, a one-man Free Trade Area of the Americas who has extensive business interests stretching from the US to Patagonia, considers Venezuela his 'backyard', where he owns the TV network Venevisión, the mobile giant Telcel and the Pepsi-Cola franchise. The Cisneros Group was deeply implicated in the 1994 Banco Latino scandal in which thousands of citizens lost their life savings due to corrupt practices (Pedro Tinoco, the bank's founder, was chairman of the Cisneros-owned Cada supermarket chain). Cisneros is also a member of the Chase Manhattan Bank's international advisory board and a close associate of Carlos Andrés Pérez. While Cisneros maintained telephone contact with top US State Department official Otto Reich during the failed coup, Isaac Pérez Recao visited both army headquarters and the presidential palace. In an April raid on Recao's Caracas home investigators uncovered uniforms, machine guns, night vision goggles, sniper paraphernalia and twelve bulletproof vests with 'Police' written on them. Recao's cache also included ID accrediting him and his wife as members of army intelligence (DIM) signed by General Ovidio Poggioli, a dissident army general.[8] Poggioli resurfaced in October 2003 as security chief for the Coordinadora Democrática as the opposition prepared to gather signatures to push for a recall referendum in early 2004.

## Aftermath

Two months after the brief coup d'etat I walked the Caracas streets in search of witnesses to the 11-A killings. No journalist, Venezuelan or otherwise, bothered to question witnesses living close to Puente Llaguno, where Chávez gunmen had allegedly fired on the opposition crowd as it arrived in the city centre.

'One of the dead men is alive,' a stranger volunteered. The voice belonged to Diogenes López, a skinny, happy-go-lucky youth, who then added in a voice suddenly thick with gravitas, 'and I am that man.' Diogenes explained how police shot him twice in the back and once in the head, upon which he was taken to hospital, declared dead and delivered to the morgue. 'But a watchman noticed I was alive,' he explained.

I began knocking on doors and, despite the reluctance of anyone to speak on the record, I found a woman living in a seventh floor apartment situated right beside the Puente Llaguno, where Chávez supporters were filmed firing at an unseen target below. The woman looked me up and down, shrugged her shoulders and spoke. 'I was looking at what was happening outside when I saw the (Metropolitan) police firing at people on the bridge.' Haydee Martinez pointed to the pockmarked walls above her head. 'The police were posted beneath the bridge.' Where were the marchers? I asked. Five blocks away, she responded – roughly three hundred metres. Martinez also saw men with rifles posted on top of the Edson Hotel, a high-rise building behind the bridge. 'I left my house for a second to help a friend caught in the crossfire,' she said. When she got back to her apartment police shrapnel sprayed the balcony, injuring her daughter. 'She still has the scars.' She called in a shy teenager who showed me the wounds on her belly. 'I'm not a Chavista,' added Haydee, 'but I recognise what he has done for the country.' Martinez is a single mother who has raised two children alone. 'I've worked since I was eleven years old,' she said, 'trying to improve myself.'

As Martinez told me her story a well-dressed man in a beige suit who had been chatting to her when I first arrived made gestures to suggest that the account I was hearing could not be trusted. José Urbina, it quickly emerged, was anti-Chávez. 'He's a disaster,' he said, 'and the dead people were all anti-Chávez'. Haydee responded angrily. 'You're an Adeco (member of Democratic Action) and you weren't even here that afternoon.'

Urbina admitted that although he lived close by he had been on the main anti-Chávez march when the shootings occurred. 'Tell him the full story,' said Martinez, as Urbina's smile grew more embarrassed. It turned out that Urbina had gone to Miraflores palace the day after the coup to cheer the coup plotters and apply for a job. He made his excuses, jumped into his car and sped off.

The Chávez supporters killed during the coup included veteran activist José Alexis González Ribete, aged 47, who was shot dead by Metropolitan Police troops in the 23 de Enero shantytown on the night of April 12th. González Ribete was an educator who had volunteered in Nicaragua during the Sandinista Revolution, working on the literacy campaign before volunteering for service in the Sandinista Army close to the Honduran border when US-backed Contra rebels launched attacks on civilian targets. 'He was a humanitarian,' said his widow, a Nicaraguan citizen who described how her murdered husband took off alone on his motorbike to rescue victims of the deadly floods in December 1999. On the night of the coup González Ribete reported to the local Bolivarian Co-ordinator and joined a group of Chávez activists who monitored events from a community building in their neighbourhood. The sound of a disturbance in a nearby carpark brought González Ribete and friends onto the streets. Alone, the veteran activist walked to the back of the car park, where he encountered a police patrol. Shots rang out and by the time Alexis's friends caught up with him he was dying, a bullet lodged in his throat. 'We never had access to the forensic results,' his widow said. An investigation into his death has led nowhere.

Luis Alberto Caro, aged 57, swore to his wife that he wouldn't go anywhere near the centre of Caracas on the day of the opposition march on April 11th, but once he heard the news that the anti-Chavistas were marching on Miraflores he left with his son Luber to 'defend the revolution.' At about 3.30pm Luber, aged 27, dived for cover. He escaped the bullets but lost contact with his father in the crowd. At 6pm that evening Luber stood to attention with other Chávez supporters for a minute's silence to honour the victims of the violence, unaware that his father was among the bodies dispatched to the morgue. A sniper's bullet to the neck left Luis Alberto Caro bleeding to death under a marquee as medical attention arrived too late to save him.

Both sides counted their dead and blamed each other for the lives lost. The anti-Chávez victims have a legal team pursuing several avenues for bringing Chávez to trial for 'crimes against humanity', while seven more victims, who were among the pro-Chávez supporters when the shooting occurred, have channelled their demands for justice through a parliamentary commission set up to investigate the events.

The subsequent looting spree also claimed more than a dozen lives. Laura Salazar was returning home with her husband and four children in their car when looters stopped them at a crossroads. A man held a gun to her husband's head and fired, leaving him in a critical state. After several medical interventions and an agonising 33-day wait, Salazar died of his wounds. The 'anti-Chávez' victims were as diverse as the rainbow march they had joined that day; many of them were taking to the streets in protest for the first time in their lives. Andrés Trujillo, an anti-Chávez protestor, recalled how he marched at the head of one section into the downtown area. 'Everyone suddenly stopped because no one knew where the presidential palace was.' The middle class rarely if ever came into the centre of town.

The 11-A investigation has since fallen victim to sectarian political point-scoring: relatives of anti-Chávez victims use their victimhood to press for Chávez's resignation while relatives of Chavista victims accuse their political enemies of organising the killings to precipitate the coup. Not even forensic evidence, dismissed as unreliable by both sides, could escape political bias. Chávez's institutional overhaul had reformed the courts, but the forensic scientists attached to anti-crime units were holdovers from the old system, which was rife with corruption. I spoke with lawyers acting on behalf of anti-Chávez victims who appeared far more interested in accumulating corpses on their 'side' than in pursuing justice for the innocent victims. 'We're still trying to get Tortoza on board,' one lawyer told me, referring to Jorge Tortoza, the 'prize' victim of 11-A, a well-known press photographer. The attempt to recruit Tortoza as a victim of state terror ultimately failed. A *New York Times* reporter spoke to Tortoza's sister Sonia Tortoza de Blanco, who described a conversation she had with her brother on the morning of the fateful events: 'Things are getting worse,' Jorge told her. 'It seems to me that they want to overthrow the government. I can't tell how this is going to end.' Sonia agreed and added, 'I can, they need at least one death', unaware of how tragically prophetic her words would become. Tortoza was posthumously named the winner of the Voices of Freedom press award given by the Venezuelan Chamber of Broadcasting and the Television Federation, which were both firmly in the anti-Chávez camp. Roberto Giusti, a prominent journalist, made a speech in Tortoza's honour: 'He was killed because he was a reporter, because his camera registered a massacre.... Tortoza was the target for all the hatred aimed at journalists.' Giusti concluded by comparing the Bolivarian defenders with 'Mussolini's fascists' while Miguel Henrique Otero, owner of *El Nacional*, recalled how he had warned the Inter-American Press Society that 'official intolerance' could lead to the death of a journalist.[9]

Anti-Chávez lawyers went on the offensive, writing their own script for the nation's history books: 'We have six victims, four dead and two injured,' lawyer Alejandro Tovar Alegrette told me. In the absence of a dead photographer the lawyers came up with a new approach, borrowed from the Bolivarian constitution they previously dismissed as a blueprint for a Stalinist dictatorship. Under Article 29 a class action suit against the government can be mounted by any number of people if they suffer stress as a result of attempted murder attributable to government negligence. Juan Sosa Azpurua, a virulent anti-Chávez lawyer, told me after a press conference that like-minded lawyers planned to gather thousands of names of people who attended the 11-A march and launch such a class action suit against Chávez. 'Then we'll have thousands of victims,' he added, with evident glee. The class action suit had no hope of prospering, conceded Azpurua, but the mere process itself would further delegitimise Chávez's adminis-tration. At the last count lawyers were attempting to prosecute Chávez for war crimes through European courts. The opposition lawyers compared the events of 11-A to Chilean dictator Augusto Pinochet's 'caravan of death', a roving death squad which executed dozens of opposition activists in the wake of the right-wing coup against Salvador Allende in September 1973. The declared anti-Chávez victims enjoyed far greater access to national and international media than those whose relatives opted to await the outcome of a parliamentary investigation. An Internet search revealed over fifty sites with information on Jesús Mohamet Capote, an eighteen-year-old murdered by a sniper's bullet as he marched with the opposi-tion. José Alexis González Ribete and Luis Alberto Caro appeared only on general victim lists, and their next of kin were absent from media reports.

## Media

'It's not information anymore, it's pure hatred.'
Octavio Azcano, from Caracas's Petare neighbourhood.

The Venezuelan media didn't just support the coup, they played a key role in the planning and execution of events as round-the-clock propaganda slots urged citizens to take to the streets and 'liberate' their country. In a startling interview conducted hours after the coup, an army general thanked a TV presenter on air for allowing the conspirators to record their message to the nation in his home. 'Now now,' tut-tutted the journalist, a little embarrassed but undeniably pleased at the acknowledgment, 'I'm just a journalist you know, just a journalist.'

The *Economist* magazine reported that Venezuela's media magnates told Carmona that they couldn't guarantee him the loyalty of the army, 'but we can promise you the support of the press.' They weren't bluffing – the nation's mainstream radio and television stations are owned by wealthy businessmen who have put their airtime at the service of the anti-Chávez cause. Even the two television channels devoted mainly to astrological shows displayed their true colours: 'I see bloodshed if Chávez doesn't leave,' said a clairvoyant on RCTV. The mass media's capitulation to the coup agenda boosted the audience for alternative media, notably antiescualidos.com a website operating out of a private apartment which attempted to break the stranglehold of the corporate media and cut through the silence imposed in the hours following the coup. In a country which enjoyed true press freedom during the Chávez administration, the hours following the coup hinted at what lay ahead under the new regime. Catia TV, located on the top floor of a hospital building, was raided on April 12th by members of the Metropolitan Police. The offices of Radio Catia Libre 93.5 FM, a community radio station, were destroyed by 15 police officers while a DJ preparing a show was detained at gunpoint and tortured in police custody. In neither case were search or arrest warrants produced. Meanwhile TV Caricuao, a community television station, was raided by police, accompanied by a Venevisión TV crew, who were promised an arms cache and militia uniforms. Nothing was found on the premises but one person was detained and beaten. Radio Perola was also searched by police without search warrants who, on finding the station empty, raided the homes of people who worked at the station. Nicolas Rivero, a station director who was detained, subsequently denounced the 'brutal torture' he underwent in custody. 'Freedom of expression is the expression of freedom and not the voice of privilege,' said Carlos Carles of Radio Perola, explaining the impulse behind the explosion of community radio and television in Venezuela.[10]

There were also some dignified voices of opposition raised within the corporate media: 'Don't report anything the Chavistas are doing,' was the order handed down to Andrés Izarra, an experienced television producer working with RCTV's flagship Observador news programme, which broadcasts three times a day with a staff of over one hundred. 'I received orders to cut the signal when the Fiscal spoke,' he told this reporter, referring to a statement of support made by the Attorney General on behalf of Chávez on the morning after the coup. Izarra described how the order came down from the station owners that 'no one linked in any way to official (Chávez) sectors' could appear on TV and their statements could not be covered on the news programme.

The station ignored the speedy street mobilisations on behalf of Chávez, an interview with Chávez's daughter Maria Gabriela in which she denounced the kidnap of her father, and an army press conference in which regional commanders expressed their loyalty and support for the ousted leader. Izarra resigned on the grounds that the TV station's behaviour violated the ethics of his profession and several articles of the constitution, which guaranteed the right to information even under state of siege legislation. 'The polarisation was bad before,' he said, 'but now we had a direct order to block out any news generated by the Chavistas.' Three months later Izarra was still out of work, blacklisted by the private TV cartel which continued to operate as an opposition party rather than a channel of information which might keep citizens informed of important events taking place in their country. In his statement to the parliamentary investigative commission, Izarra concluded that Venezuela's four private TV channels effectively forfeited their right to broadcast; Venezuela's constitution permits the recall of the president halfway through his period in office yet there is no provision for the revocation of television licences.

Chávez's cautious inquiry into media accountability procedures earned him a harsh rebuke from the Committee for the Protection of Journalists and other press watchdog groups, who labelled any regulation efforts an attack on press freedom.[11] The Inter-American Press Society (*Sociedad Interamericana de la Prensa*, SIP) awarded its 2003 media prize to Venezuelan journalists for 'not caving into government harassment … for fulfilling its duty to inform in times of crisis … journalists risking their lives, facing danger and intimidation from the government for expressing themselves freely.' It came as no surprise that the SIP award was shared with Cuba's independent media, who had been harassed and imprisoned by Fidel Castro's government.[12] The attempt to link Castro's repressive media policy with Venezuela's remarkable press freedom was a crude propaganda exercise by an organisation which has historically bowed to US foreign policy dictat. 'Freedom of press does not exist in Venezuela,' said Jorge Fascetto, former SIP president, currently president of the International Press Institute, speaking at the 33rd assembly of the Organisation of American States (OAS).

However, it would be unfair to single out the Venezuelan media as the sole responsible agent for the distortion of events. Respected international media performed the task with equal skill. In an April 13 editorial, the *New York Times* triumphantly declared that Chávez's 'resignation' meant that 'Venezuelan democracy is no longer threatened by a would-be dictator.' Conspicuously avoiding the word 'coup', the *Times* explained that Chávez 'stepped down after the military intervened and handed power to a respected business leader.' The Chicago *Tribune's* editorial board was highly impressed by the coup. An April 14 editorial called Chávez an 'elected strongman' and declared: 'It's not every day that a democracy benefits from the military's intervention to force out an elected president.' The *Tribune* hoped that Venezuela could 'move on to better things' now that the tyrant was 'safely out of power and under arrest.' No longer would Chávez be free to pursue his habits of 'toasting Fidel Castro, flying to Baghdad to visit Saddam Hussein, or praising Osama bin Laden.' When US media watchdog Fairness and Accuracy in the Media (FAIR) called the *Tribune* to check the reference to Chávez's habitual praise for Bin Laden, the author of the piece, *Tribune* editorial board member Steve Chapman, said that in attempting to locate the reference for FAIR, he discovered that he had 'misread' his source.[13] There was no apology for the alarming misrepresentation.

International human rights monitors at the Committee for the Protection of Journalists (CPJ) and Human Rights Watch (HRW) replicated the blindness of the Inter-American Press Society, seeing only repressive intent in Chávez's relationship with the media. In the wake of the coup the Chávez administration prepared legislation to punish incitement to hatred, bringing the country into line with European legislation. 'A very grave step backwards,' said HRW chief José Miguel Vivanco, ignoring the Venezuelan media's key role in orchestrating a coup d'etat and the suppression of information gathered by its own reporters. There is no government in the world which allows liberal press freedom laws to be used as a vehicle for incitement to hatred or for the overthrow of the state.

The Venezuelan media's dull diet of anti-Chávez propaganda has inspired the growth of alternative media outlets, from badly-typed handouts to glossy magazines and community television. There have also been initiatives by media workers themselves, attempting to redress the balance. 'Journalists for Truth' was established in January 2003, pledging to 'rescue journalism' from media owners that 'oblige their staff to offer visibly distorted information.' The new organisation is made up of media workers involved in all aspects of radio, print and television work. Meanwhile *Los del Medio* (literally 'those of the media' but also a play on the word *medio* which also means the middle) launched a watchdog group pledged to monitor abuses by both sides. The opposition media has logged dozens of 'aggressions' ranging from verbal threats to terror attacks, but the alleged incidents appear to be driven more by a desire for publicity than any real and imminent threat to the lives of media commentators.

Nevertheless, journalists in Venezuela today face constant physical risks. Human Rights Watch estimates that there were at least 130 assaults and threats of physical harm to journalists and press property between the beginning of 2002 and February 2003, and the assaults continue. It is not the government, the police or the armed forces that commit these acts of aggression, however, but civilians who strongly identify with the president and his proclaimed revolutionary programme – much street graffiti in Caracas attests that a significant segment of the population is angered by the press. Many feel that the media has failed to do its essential job of providing the public with accurate and unbiased information. Both members of the government and their civilian supporters who mount angry vigils outside the television studios share this view. Many journalists interviewed by Human Rights Watch themselves had deep misgivings about the political role the press is currently playing in Venezuela.[14]

The US media wasn't the only sector to declare its support for the coup plotters; US taxpayers also funded the conspiracy through State Department grants to conservative organisations. Over US$1 million in public funds was released to the National Endowment for Democracy (NED) to boost opposition groups in Venezuela. The US government even facilitated the opening of a 'democratic transition' office in Caracas, a mechanism generally reserved for countries moving from an authoritarian to a democratic system.[15]

The government named a parliamentary commission to investigate the events of 11-A. A restricted document, seen by this reporter, revealed a list of 75 victims and witnesses of the 11-A violence, assembled during the state investigation. The list included seven murdered government supporters, dozens of injured and a group of witnesses who described what they saw from vantage points close to the action. The description of the circumstances surrounding the dead and injured were predictably brief: 'Nelson Zambrano died of a bullet wound in the thorax in the vicinity of the Palacio Blanco'; 'Pedro Jose Linares died of a firearm wound in the thorax and through internal haemorraging. He was with the (Chávez) crowd at Miraflores.' There were other deaths during the looting in the hours following the coup, and a dozen people injured during the chaos named the Metropolitan Police as their aggressors. I met several people who had suffered shrapnel injuries from Metropolitan Police bullets but they were too afraid to publicly denounce their attackers. The forensic evidence later implicated 38 members of the Metropolitan Police force who, it was determined, had discharged their weapons at short range against the Chávez supporters posted on the Puente Llaguno. At least three Chávez supporters were killed by Metropolitan Police fire. The police dismissed the evidence as biased but photos subsequently revealed Metropolitan Police officers firing machine guns and non-regulation hand weapons.

The agony continued for some families, with Orlando Rojas, a health worker inside the presidential palace, dying after a 65-day battle with his injuries. A year after the 11-A events several of the wounded were still in Cuba, where they received free medical attention for severe wounds. Weeks later, at the end of a pro-Chávez rally in Avenida Bolívar, I sat drinking coffee in a bakery when a Metropolitan Police officer pulled up on a motor bike. He looked around at the Chávez supporters, looked at me and then said in a loud voice: '*Animales salvajes!*' (Savage animals!) 'They shouldn't be allowed into the city centre.' I was astonished at the outburst, and waited for a reaction from the Chávez supporters, who outnumbered the law enforcement officer by twenty to one. They simply ignored the comments, evidently accustomed to the abuse. The police official then introduced himself – Sergeant Franklin Reverón, 'Director of Operations' – and gave me his mobile phone number. (Interested readers in Europe can dial 00-58-414-3398697 and ask Señor Reverón for personal tips on law enforcement.) 'Are you working with the US Embassy?' he asked me, before speeding away on his motorbike. The incident was a one-off chance encounter and may not reflect the feelings of the police as a whole, but the vitriol was unnerving. It came as no surprise to discover that in July 2003 an angry group of Petare residents destroyed a police booth in their barrio after officers attacked Chávez supporters who faced down an opposition demonstration. 'We're sick and tired of their abuses,' said one resident as the National Guard moved in, to the sound of cheers from the community.

Three months after 11-A, three 'special delegates' named by Attorney General Isaías Rodríguez delivered their verdict on the investigation to date: 'Over the past two months we have witnessed with preoccupation that the events of April have generated opinions which, far from pursuing reconciliation and justice, seek to exacerbate confrontation through confusion and manipulation.' Father Juan Vives Suria, a Salesian priest and member of the monitoring group, urged both sides not to use the victims as a tool for their own ambitions to power.

## International reaction

Chávez's presidential colleagues around Latin America formally condemned 'the interruption of constitutional order' at a meeting of the 19-nation Rio Group of Latin American countries, which happened to be meeting on the weekend the coup occurred. However the first reaction of regional leaders and diplomats revealed widespread sympathy for the short-lived coup: 'It's up to the Venezuelans,' said Mexican president Vicente Fox, on first hearing of it. 'They've made their decision, there's a new government, they have the right to make their own decisions.'[16] Colombia's acting foreign minister also rushed to support the coup: 'We hope to have the best of relations with the transition government,' said Clemencia Forero, who described Carmona as a 'good friend' of Colombia. Chilean president Ricardo Lagos was forced to remove his ambassador in Caracas, Marcos Alvarez, who expressed his satisfaction with the overthrow of the Chávez administration. 'The new president (Carmona) has excellent relations with Chile,' boasted the ambassador, who took the opportunity to praise the democratic spirit of the Venezuelan people. 'This was no coup d'etat,' he said, adding, 'I'm impressed by the tranquillity and civility of the people, steeped in democracy over the past forty years.' The ambassador made one final reflection, thinking perhaps of his own country's flawed institutions: 'democracy, as we know, is imperfect, but it's still democracy.'

The US Government was also enthusiastic at the turn of events as White House spokesman Ari Fleischer confidently announced the resignation of Chávez: 'There was a peaceful demonstration, people exercised their right to protest, Chávez supporters fired on the people and that quickly led to the situation in which Chávez resigned.' For good measure Fleischer added that before signing himself out as president, Chávez 'sacked his vice-president and cabinet.' This was the justification that the coup was legal, as Carmona could only take office if the vice-president had absented himself.

On his reinstatement to office Chávez was asked whether the US might have had a role in the failed coup. 'God forbid,' he replied. 'It would be extremely harmful for international stability and for democracies around the world.'[17] In a comment made to this journalist a short time before the coup

Chávez was more candid: 'No one can deny it, history has documented it, how the US backed the destabilisation of Allende's government, the blockade of Cuba, the invasion of Guatemala, the invasion of Panama, the Dominican Republic, Haiti, Grenada.' Yet Chávez remained optimistic that US policy had moved on: 'I prefer to think, as we enter the 21$^{st}$ century, that those in power in the US, especially those with an eye on Latin America, are aware of the tremendous threats in the region, I refer to the threat of poverty, the greatest threat to democratic systems everywhere and the seeds of future violence.'

The current Bush administration is awash with veteran right-wing officials who interpret service to their country as a licence to destabilise democratic governments in order to improve the investment climate for corporate clients. Cuban-Americans occupy seven out of twelve key posts in the government's Latin America Department, part of a neo-conservative clique described as having 'all the intolerant instincts of a weird American religious cult, impervious to any criticism of their fantasy picture of Iraq, the Middle East and the rest of the world.'[18] In June 2002 I attended the first mass mobilisation of Chávez supporters since the April coup attempt. The streets were packed with at least half a million people – even perhaps twice that figure, it was impossible to tell. The majority were poor and wore the red beret that symbolises unconditional loyalty to Chávez. 'Do you believe in God?' one government supporter asked me, 'because a man without God is incomplete.' Another man railed against divorce while countless Che Guevara t-shirts paid tribute to armed struggle and makeshift stalls were set up to explain aspects of the Bolivarian constitution. The Chavista phenomenon appeared more a matter of personal faith than ideological conviction, with supporters searching for something to hold on to in times of extreme uncertainty.

## Coordinadora Democrática

Venezuela's Democratic Co-ordinator (*Coordinadora Democrática*, CD) is an umbrella opposition group comprising political parties, employer and labour groups and NGOs hostile to President Chávez's political project. The Co-ordinator came together to strengthen opposition efforts in the run-up to the April 2002 coup. The parties range from the extreme left (*Bandera Roja*) to extreme right (*Primero Justicia*) and have united around the single goal of ousting Chávez from power. The Democratic Co-ordinator is recognised by government and international bodies alike as the legal representative of the disparate opposition forces. The CD co-ordinated the Gran Toma Cívica de Caracas at which millions of signatures were collected to push for a recall referendum against Chávez. When the National Electoral Council declared the first signature-gathering process invalid, the Co-ordinator organised the 'Reafirmazo' for late November, hoping to gather sufficient signatures to force a recall vote halfway through the presidential period.

When I asked a political analyst who the Coordinadora leader was he told me, only half jokingly, 'Hugo Chávez.' The Venezuelan president's removal is the sole object of the CD's existence. The organisation's diverse membership is held together precisely by its opposition to Chávez and the realisation (aided by numerous opinion polls) that no single opposition candidate could beat Chávez at the polls should fresh presidential elections occur. If the elections were held tomorrow, 39 per cent of Venezuelans say they would opt for Chávez, while no opposition candidate polls more than 18 per cent. A unified candidate running on an anti-Chávez platform would have a chance of defeating the incumbent, but the Co-ordinator has tremendous divisions lurking just beneath the surface that would be exploited on the campaign trail by Chávez.

Like all opposition efforts, the CD bases its legitimacy on the Bolivarian Constitution, invoking article 350, which gives citizens the right to 'disown any government which abuses fundamental rights.' The weakness of the CD is its insistence that a single show of strength by the opposition should be sufficient grounds to force Chávez to resign office. In April 2002, the huge march that preceded the failed coup was considered evidence enough that Chávez had lost his popular mandate. By December, the economic paralysis arising from the oil strike and the accompanying mobilisations were also considered grounds for the ousting of Chávez. The CD also bases its legitimacy on opinion polls and studies commissioned by influential business groups out to overthrow the Chávez administration. In August 2003 the handover of 2.5 million signatures, or 20 per cent of the electorate, was considered sufficient to demand that Chávez resign. The CD made desultory attempts at a series of mobilisations – the tour of popular neighbourhoods in mid-2003, for instance, designed to show Chávez that the poor areas regarded as Bolivarian strongholds were no longer in the hands of his supporters. But the result was a disaster. At the *Guairazo*, a mobilisation held in la Guaira, less than one thousand people showed up after round-the-clock media coverage and media estimates anticipated a 15,000-strong turnout. I was in attendance and several people acknowledged, when pressed on the issue, that they had been bussed in from a neighbouring state in return for lunch and a few dollars.

In fact, the CD is a temporary alliance of unlikely bedfellows which has delayed the real work of building a long-term electoral alternative to the Chávez administration. The latest organising plan of the Co-ordinator is to travel door to door to collect millions of signatures against Chávez. The yawning abyss between a signature given to a campaigning neighbour and a political project aimed at improving the living standards of Venezuelans has been filled by the nation's omnipresent media – the single greatest obstacle to reconciliation in this divided nation.

By August 2002 the Venezuelan opposition felt confident enough to restart its campaign to oust the president, once more confusing their obsessive dislike of Chávez with the general mood of the population. The minor issue of the coup debâcle was brushed aside as a matter of Pedro Carmona's poor political judgement. The opposition leaders refused to acknowledge Chávez's mandate: 'He won't survive a couple of puffs of air,' said CTV president Carlos Ortega. 'His only option is to resign.'[19] Human Rights Watch reported its concern that 'some opposition sectors still consider unconstitutional methods to resolve the crisis.' On the issue of press freedom, HRW acknowledged that 'everyone here says what they like, how they like it.' Finally, the dissident colonel who marched in public wearing his uniform was criticised in the report on the grounds that 'using an army uniform is not the same as wearing a postman's outfit.'[20] A fortnight later, on the eve of an opposition rally, the CTV leadership speculated on how quickly Chávez could be removed from power: 'If one million people turn out on the march today,' said General-Secretary Manuel Cova, 'then Chávez will have to abandon office.'[21] The employers' federation once more offered a day's wages to every worker who attended the march.[22] A group of international observers, including European and US diplomats, were invited to monitor the march, highlighting the growing international involvement in the unfolding scenario. President Chávez spoke on national television, wishing the protestors good luck while calling on security forces to act with restraint. In an effort to pursue dialogue with the opposition he called on the Venezuelan Episcopal Conference to intercede, despite that institution's public disapproval of the Chávez administration.

Meanwhile, former Supreme Court president Cecilia Sosa resurfaced long enough to call on Venezuelan citizens to disobey the laws of the land. 'No one is calling his (Chávez) legitimacy into question,' conceded Sosa. 'But he doesn't know how to administer the *hacienda*,' she added, referring to the large ranches dotted around the country.[23] It was a revealing word to have chosen – the term 'hacienda' echoed a phrase used by dictator Juan Vicente Gómez, who boasted about how his ability to run his own hacienda gave him the experience to run Venezuela, which he viewed as simply a bigger version of his own ranch. Sosa suggested that dissatisfied citizens form *juntas ciudadanas* (citizen committees) to combat the Bolivarian Circles. The juntas would meet each week and decide which laws they would ignore. It was notable that the first proposal of the disobedience juntas was the non-payment of income tax, an instrument which applied almost exclusively to the middle and upper classes. (The poor were already taxed to the hilt through VAT on basic goods and services.) Once more the opposition turned to the Bolivarian constitution to defend actions that would have landed them in prison under the previous 1961 constitution. In that document, Article 66 outlawed 'propaganda which encouraged ... the disobeying of laws.' Chávez's constitution suppressed this article and added article 62 which encouraged citizens to repudiate 'unjust laws'. Meanwhile Article 350 protected civil disobedience in cases where such activity is taken 'in loyalty to the constitution and the principles underpinning it.' The opposition argued that Chávez had assumed authoritarian powers and approved the 49 laws to the detriment of the nation while failing to protect citizen rights during protests.[24]

The 11-A coup brought Chávez's hardline opponents out of the closet and into the limelight just long enough for the ousted government to take note of the treachery. The events boosted Chávez's more radical supporters, who called for the acceleration of the revolutionary process. The coup also showed how strong the opposition was and how far it was willing to go to achieve its goal of replacing Chávez. The coup consolidated Chávez's authority inside army barracks and in poor neighbourhoods where citizens risked their lives to take to the streets and ensure the return of their president. The coup was defeated but Chávez opted not to move against all but the most visible leaders of the conspiracy. The absence of sanctions against the opposition was interpreted as a sign of government weakness. The Venezuelan Supreme Court subsequently overruled a magistrate's order to try four senior army officers implicated in the coup, ruling that the events of 11-A did not constitute a coup d'etat but a 'power vacuum'.[25] Chávez disagreed with the ruling but made no attempt to interfere with the verdict.

The coup plotters regrouped and planned their next move against Chávez amid speculation that an assassination attempt might come next, but in the end it seems the spectre of a bloody civil war was too much for even the extreme right to stomach. The example of Jorge Eliecer Gaitán, Colombia's popular presidential candidate, murdered in Bogotá on the campaign trail in April 1948, may have served as a cautionary tale. His murder unleashed a wave of violence which led to 250,000 deaths between 1948 and 1951. It was no coincidence that on the first anniversary of the April 2002 coup attempt, Chávez invited Gaitán's grand-daughter to be the guest of honour.

Historically, Venezuela's armed forces had been the first great hope of coup plotters, the most effective short-cut to power. Attention now turned to the nation's 'jugular' – the oil industry.

## Oil

While the youthful Hugo Chávez plotted secretly in the barracks in 1982, a parallel clandestine project with very different goals yet a similar self-justification was underway inside oil giant PDVSA. Just as elements inside the armed forces believed they could govern the country more efficiently than the nation's corrupt political class, so too did PDVSA's 'oil generals' believe they had a divine right to administer the country's massive oil revenues, which they viewed as having been squandered by short-sighted government policies.

The oil industry had been nationalised in 1976; it would play a crucial role in financing President Carlos Andrés Pérez's 'Agenda Venezuela', an industrialisation plan based on expanded oil revenues. The plan proved a disaster, however, as corruption and pilferage wasted oil monies. PDVSA management executives conspired to retain oil revenues and invest them outside the country where they would be beyond the reach of the government. Since the nationalization of the oil industry in 1976 Venezuelan governments have ironically had progressively less influence in defining oil policy. Foreign oil giants Exxon, Shell and Gulf groomed Venezuelan executives to occupy senior posts in advance of the nationalisation process. PDVSA's Board of Directors quickly succeeded in reducing the role of the Ministry of Energy and Mines in policy formulation until it finally became little more than a rubber stamp. The plausible pretext was that the industry needed to be protected from the threat of irresponsible political clientelism. The impulse for a policy designed to limit profits was the decision of the Herrera administration in 1983 to use $5 million of PDVSA currency reserves to stave off devaluation. From then on, the resources generated by PDVSA were increasingly invested abroad, buying refineries and even a chain of service stations in the United States. An independent audit of the firm carried out under the Chávez administration revealed that many of the assets bought were not good business. It also revealed the extent to which PDVSA has used transfer pricing to favour its foreign subsidiaries and limit its own declared profits. In the case of the Citgo service stations these subsidies have been passed on to consumers by offering the cheapest petrol prices available in the United States. But these foreign subsidiaries never transferred profits to PDVSA and consequently never contributed taxes to the Venezuelan treasury.

As might be expected when foreign companies controlled oil production and fixed the price per barrel of crude, the state kept a close eye on proceedings. Once the oil industry was nationalised, however, congress no longer deemed such vigilance necessary and took the extraordinary step of granting president Andrés Pérez discretionary rights over the spending of oil revenues. Such monies increased from $1.4 billion per year in 1970 to $9 billion in 1974, encouraging Pérez to borrow against future profits to finance his 'Great Venezuela' project. The oil generals in PDVSA oriented policy toward consumer countries, breaking OPEC quotas in the belief that economic policy was based on attracting foreign investment. PDVSA was transformed into a 'state within the state', as secretive as any large corporation, but with the difference that its secrets were not even shared with the owner of the company, in this case the government.

By 1989 PDVSA management was acting like a global corporation, sharing the same interests as foreign oil companies pressing for the elimination of obstacles to outside investment in natural resources, a position that found support among Venezuelan professionals and the middle class. Small wonder that *Time* Magazine named PDVSA president Luis Giusti 'Manager of the Year'. (Giusti is a wealthy private owner of oil tankers and computer services, and the chief architect behind the internationalization of the firm during the Rafael Caldera administration. He was subsequently appointed by the White House as an advisor on US energy policy.) The PDVSA management strategy had seen oil prices tumble to $9 a barrel in 1998, but Chávez's election coincided with the tripling of oil prices that created $29 billion in oil income in 2000 as Chávez revitalised OPEC and sought ways to keep crude at a solid price between $22 and $28 per barrel. The Ministry of Energy and Mines, ignored by PDVSA executives before Chávez, sharpened its teeth under the stewardship of Ali Rodríguez, former president of the congressional committee on energy and mines (1994–97), which monitored contracts arising from the opening up of the oil industry to foreign markets. Under

Chávez, Rodríguez's first task was to reassert the primacy of his ministry over PDVSA, which had become 'a vast conglomerate dispensing favours and bribes.'[26] Rodriguez began to monitor the volume produced in the fields and rejected the transfer pricing system that allowed PDVSA to evade its fiscal responsibilities. Despite the myth of an efficient 'meritocracy' working for the good of the nation, PDVSA remained a bloated white elephant operating on the basis of 'better a dollar spent than a dollar paid in taxes.' All along the production chain costs were maximised to reduce revenues that might end up in state hands.

In November 2001 Chávez approved a new Law of Hydro-carbons, aimed at reclaiming effective state control over PDVSA. The new law required the company to present separate accounts, a method designed to cast light on the secret activities of the oil elite. The new oil law also reformed investment rules in Venezuela, but contrary to opposition claims it also stimulated foreign investment and opened the nation's sacred national asset to outside investment. Among the provisions of the new law was 51 per cent public ownership of new oil ventures. Up until then investors had to pay 67 per cent in income taxes and 16.6 per cent in royalty taxes. According to the new framework, income tax was reduced to 50 per cent while royalty taxes were increased by up to 30 per cent. The new laws did not affect contracts approved by the pre-Chávez parliament. Also, for the first time in history, the law provided for legal private participation with the production of crude oil, from zero under the former law, to 49 per cent.[27] The row building up over reforms to the oil industry gained pace in the months following the coup, providing the focus for the next major mobilisation against Chávez. PDVSA's dissident managers relied heavily on the company's reputation for efficiency and technical capacity, a corporate administration run along 'meritocratic' lines, allowing the most talented to rise to the top. This idealised image was dented by international business statistics for 2000. PDVSA remained at the top of Latin America's top 50 business chart, competing as an equal with global oil giants Texaco and Shell. However, when productivity was compared to other companies, the picture seemed less positive. Texaco generated $1.9 million per worker per year, while Exxon turned over $1.8 million, Shell $1.6 million. The figure for PDVSA employees was just $770,000. In comparison with its oil-producing neighbours, an examination of 'profits on sales' left Petroecuador in 2nd place with 85 per cent, Petrobras number 32 with 20 per cent and PDVSA trailing in 49th place with 13.7 per cent. The technical competence of PDVSA employees was beyond doubt, but problems arose in administration as the company carried an inflated workforce and a top-heavy management payroll.[28]

The approval of the Law on Hydrocarbons offered a legal basis for reforming PDVSA but also set the stage for major political and economic confrontation. When Chávez returned to office after the coup he backed down on the PDVSA leadership issue, permitting the reinstatement of ousted executives. Ali Rodríguez assumed the Presidency of PDVSA with the task of persuading the executive team to accompany the government. Not surprisingly, Rodríguez was unable to reconcile the dissident executives with the government's new oil policy, a failure which led to the crippling work stoppage of December 2002.

## The oligarchy strikes back (December 2002–March 2003)

The oligarchy struck back at Chávez with the best card in its hand – foreign and private investment. Private investment contracted by 18 per cent in 1999 and barely rose in 2000 while the country's currency reserves dropped by 20 per cent in the first half of 2001, despite the boom in oil revenues. An estimated 900,000 citizens rose above the poverty line in 2000 thanks to the sharp rise in oil revenues.[29] There was massive capital outflow as an estimated $8 billion departed the country in the first 18 months of government. The state education budget increased from 3.3 to 5.2 per cent of GNP between 1999 and 2001, while the share for public housing and community services rose from 0.8 to 1.5 per cent and health spending from 1.1 to 1.4 per cent. The middle class has little reason to appreciate these advances, since it relied on private schools and medical treatment.

Chávez reinstituted the unpopular value-added tax which his predecessor had abolished in 1994 but rolled back efforts to privatise the national pension system. Chávez's support was by now predominantly among the majority poor, and the glue holding their support together was the prospect of short-term improvements to their living standards. Constant rumours of an attempt to overthrow the government paralysed the administration as the threat of strikes and violence once more dominated the political scenario.

In October 2002 a 12-hour protest strike tested the waters for a more sustained push against Chávez. The strike was successful among private business and affiliated labour unions, but did not affect the flow of oil, the key factor in keeping the economy afloat. Hardly a week passed by without a fresh call to rebellion by some sector of the security forces as Chávez struggled to assert control over the police force. In November 2002 the government intervened in the Metropolitan Police, a partisan force linked to opposition mayor Alfredo Peña. The commissioner of the force, Henry Vivas, was replaced by Gonzalo Sánchez Delgado while troops monitored police stations after a violent incident between pro- and anti-Chávez officers left two dead and twenty more injured. The immediate cause of the confrontation was a dispute over pay, but it was clear that pro- and anti-Chávez divisions were what really determined the pace of confrontation. Caracas mayor Alfredo Peña disowned the new authorities and ordered police officers to disobey them, urging the 7,000-strong force to rebellion.[30]

These events were closely followed by an 'uprising' of 14 senior army officers led by General Enrique Medina Gómez, who declared a public square in the affluent Altamira neighbourhood 'territory liberated by the institutional armed forces.' The generals and admirals were active officers suspended in the wake of their suspected participation in the April coup. Their numbers swelled to over one hundred. Once more relying on the Bolivarian constitution – which they professed to despise – the dissidents cited an article that permits citizens to 'refuse to recognise any regime which contradicts their democratic values and principles.' (At this point Chávez could have been regretting his decision to order a copy of the Bolivarian constitution sent to every home in the country.)

The establishment of a permanent rebel army camp at a busy city centre plaza was Venezuela's answer to the classic *foco guerrillero*, an act of provocation which challenged Chávez's authority in a sensitive area: army pride. José Vicente Rangel, vice-president, dismissed the rebel generals as 'clowns who commanded neither troops nor loyalty,' an opinion vindicated over the following weeks as the rebellion failed to spark support inside the barracks, as in the wake of the April coup Chávez had promoted loyal officers to senior posts. Meanwhile, the Organisation of American States (OAS), which took an increasingly active role in the search for a mediated consensus, condemned the dissident troops, stating that the 'attitudes and demands (of the rebel officers) betray the constitutional loyalty that officials of the armed forces owe to president Chávez.' Chávez opted to ignore this provocative protest, which might have gained momentum had he forcibly removed the soldiers from the square. 'We are not going until Chávez resigns,' one of the generals told the media, once more underestimating the ability of the nation's resourceful and stubborn leader.[31]

At the time of writing, the rebel army camp at Plaza Francia consisted of a handful of dissidents observed by elderly ladies walking their dogs. Back then, however, the tents and tables gave the misleading impression that the dissident troops were dug in like officers in the battlefield – when in fact most members of the group were sleeping in donated apartments in the luxurious high-rise condominiums that ring the square. The comforts undoubtedly helped the officers maintain their perfectly pressed uniforms and brilliantly polished shoes while business was brisk in flags and frying pans and, for the busy citizen, recordings of the pot-banging protests: 'I have my own cassette of it,' confessed Armando Lefmans. 'You put it on at a high volume so you don't have to bother hitting a pan.'[32]

There was a glimmer of hope in December 2002, when Brazilian Worker's Party candidate Luiz Inácio Lula da Silva won a resounding second round presidential election victory, securing 51 million voters, or 61 per cent of the electorate. President Chávez had openly expressed his support for Lula in the previous months, considering the former metal worker an ideological ally. Top Chávez officials commented privately that the election of Lula was a matter of life and death for Chávez, who badly needed a powerful ally in the region. Members of the popular movement in Latin America pointed to Chávez, Lula and Lucio Gutiérrez of Ecuador as evidence of a shift toward the left and the emergence of an alternative power bloc critical of the Washington Consensus. However, while Chávez had pinned his ideological colours to the mast, it seemed unlikely that Lula or Gutiérrez had any appetite for fighting the same battle. Ecuadorian president Lucio Gutiérrez, known as the 'Ecuadorian Chávez', relied on the indigenous movement Pachakutic to launch his electoral bid for office. Once in power, however, Gutiérrez prioritised negotiations with the IMF, wooed support in Washington and reneged on his campaign pledge to review state permission for a US military base. After six months of co-government, Pachakutic withdrew support from the governing coalition and at the movement's third congress in September 2003 the 650 delegates from around the country declared 'total opposition' to Gutiérrez. Meanwhile in Brazil, after 100 days in office President Lula had convinced conservative sceptics that his regime would play by pre-established rules. As one reporter noted, 'economic indicators are greatly improved after Lula not only stuck to his promise of moderation but surprised many by taking a more conservative path than his neo-liberal predecessor.'[33] Pedro Ribeiro of the National Conference of Brazilian Bishops said that 'the trust of the popular movements is still great, since Lula is seen as a comrade on the same journey.' But Ribeiro also warned that 'discomfort with economic policy is growing.' The dilemma faced by Chávez was now replicated in Brazil and Ecuador: structural reform implemented on behalf of the poor came with a guarantee of hostility from the business sector tied to inter-national financial interests. In the case of Lula and Gutiérrez, both leaders assumed office with a parliamentary minority, obliging them to accept compromise and consensus on all aspects of their political programmes.

Venezuelan business and union leaders called a general strike for December 2nd 2002, and a massive signature-gathering day on December 4th to press for a referendum on Chávez's rule. The double action would combine a civic insurrection on the streets with a legitimising action at the polls in an attempt to pave the way for Chávez's ousting. The Venezuelan leader won his first election in 1998 by a comfortable margin, but four out of ten voters nonetheless rejected his political vision from the beginning. Four years later, opposition had grown as the leader's controversial reform programme alienated even some of his own support base. The ruling MVR had seen its parliamentary majority whittled down from over two dozen to just four or five seats. Many citizens, once indifferent to Chávez, now feared the prospect of permanent civil strife as long as he remained in power. The political atmosphere within the ranks of the MVR, dominated by yes-people anxious to bolster the caudillo, was described as an 'ideological monoculture' which narrowed the Bolivarian revolution's support base.[34]

President Chávez egged on the hardline opposition: 'I challenge the opposition to stop the country. Let's see if they can. Go on, do it.' His enemies were dismissed as 'fascist, coup-plotting elites', which, on the evidence of the previous coup attempt, was certainly true. Public opinion would be guided by the effectiveness of the strike action as an economic shutdown would affect vast sectors of the population. Pressure would then grow on Chávez to end the strike before the economy weakened further, obliging him to opt for repression or resignation. The popular leader had shown no appetite for repression, neither during nor after the April coup attempt, which increased opposition confidence. The business, union and media chiefs gambled on an all-out strike combined with permanent street mobilisation to produce an 'insurrectionary atmosphere' that would force Chávez to step down in a matter of days.

The general strike enjoyed success in areas dominated by private business with distribution and transport initially paralysed. On day two the strike waned, but the electoral authorities gave the green light for a consultative referendum to be held on February 2nd 2003, a boost to the anti-Chávez camp. There were scuffles and tear gas as National Guard troops cleared blocked highways and tackled protestors outside oil company offices. On day three a huge opposition march reminded Chávez that the streets he once owned were now disputed by an increasingly daring opposition, while the oil industry began grinding to a halt, threatening the survival of the government. The march ended at the Hotel Melía, where OAS president César Gaviria brokered fruitless talks between government and opposition delegates. The events that mattered, however, were taking place on the streets of Caracas as pro- and anti-Chávez supporters engaged in daily street battles.

As for the presence of the OAS president, the attempt to bring government and opposition elements into dialogue with each other had begun soon after the April coup but foundered amidst mutual accusations of bad faith. Jimmy Carter visited Venezuela in July 2002, meeting all parties to the conflict but failing to get them to meet each other. The Carter initiative was doomed from the beginning; the former US president's rapport with Cuban leader Fidel Castro guaranteed suspicion among hardline anti-Chávez groups. The opposition demanded OAS mediation, which was reluctantly accepted by Chávez, who was well aware of the pro-US bias of the institution.

The dispute centred on Chávez's permanence in office as the opposition demanded nothing short of resignation or, failing that, that the February referendum be given the status of a recall vote. If Chávez lost then he would be obliged to stand down. The new constitution did not permit a recall referendum until halfway through the president's mandate – in this case August 19th 2003. The Chávez administration was in no mood for compromise on the issue, outraged that the opposition were once more trying to achieve through bullying tactics what they had failed to achieve at the election booth.

The conflict turned bloody on Friday December 6th, day four of the strike, when a gunman of Portuguese origin opened fire indiscriminately on dissident officers camped inside Plaza Francia, killing eight people and injuring dozens more. The self-confessed killer, João de Gouveia, aged 39, made no attempt to escape from the crime scene. He was subsequently tried and imprisoned for life but never revealed any motive for the killing spree. By day eight of the strike the situation had turned critical: there were daily violent street confrontations, and citizens engaged in panic-buying of basic goods, fearing an end to supplies. The oil industry ground to a virtual halt as PDVSA management resigned en masse amidst government claims of sabotage by departing executives. Luis Miquilena, once a staunch Chávez ally, abandoned the government over the 49 laws and his comments set the tone for the days ahead: 'There can be no turning back, Chávez must fall.' The US restarted the campaign against Chávez as Richard Boucher, spokesman for Colin Powell, urged Chávez to announce early elections. In addition the Bush administration advised US nationals to leave the country as talk turned to the increasing risk of a bloody civil war.[35] On the same day Chávez ordered the National Guard to protect oil refineries and the filling stations that remained open as production dropped to a third of normal output. Banks closed their doors but were threatened with fines by the government, as established under the new *Ley de Bancos*, one of the 49 laws.

Opposition protests were matched by massive pro-government shows of strength while restaurant owners in middle-class areas were threatened with violence and boycott if they refused to close their doors and join the strike. Customs officers joined the strike, schools closed their doors and alcohol grew scarce as the powerful Polar beverage conglomerate backed the strike. All eyes turned to the armed forces as dissident soldiers maintained their camp in Plaza Francia and urged their comrades to abandon the government. This time, however, the army was better informed of events on the ground and refused to be drawn into a conflict engineered to advance the coup plotters' ambitions. The armed forces commander general Julio José Garcia Montoya denounced the 'psychological warfare' conducted by the media, designed, he claimed, to confuse the population and draw the army into the conflict.

The tug of war continued between the two sides, with a glint of hope appearing on day sixteen of the strike when the OAS declared its 'full support' for Venezuela's democratic institutions and 'categorically rejected' any attempt to subvert the constitutional order presided over by Hugo Chávez. The opposition had expected the government to collapse within days of embarking on strike action, while Chávez in turn anticipated a speedy collapse of the upper-class strike, which was more an employer lockout than a worker-led initiative. The dramatic turnaround during the April coup and the undemocratic behaviour of the opposition had cooled international support for the coup plotters, and foreign governments cautiously observed the unfolding events. The US Government, however, appeared to throw in its lot with the radical opposition once more, advising Chávez that 'the only peaceful and politically viable path out of the crisis is through the holding of early elections.' The Chávez administration politely admonished the White House, reminding them that any poll before the halfway point in the presidential period would be unconstitutional. The US immediately backed down on the issue.

The launch of the general strike coincided with a painful defection from Chávez's side when his wife Marisabel publicly separated from her husband. In addition, the first lady made a public appeal for Chávez to reconsider his policies: 'In the name of your daughter, listen to the people,' said Marisabel, interviewed on a radio station in her native Barquisimeto province. Marisabel had been an elected delegate to the constitutional assembly that rewrote the constitution in 1999, but once the pressure began she steadily withdrew from public life. 'I don't want to be a martyr of the revolution or to be used as a political object by the opposition,' she said, attempting to steer a middle course. The sound of pots banging outside her home was audible during the interview as opposition activists still regarded her as an enemy. Marisabel had first abandoned the presidential palace earlier in the year when constant pot banging and hostile, spitting crowds made life unbearable for herself and her young daughter. 'There they are, Señor Presidente, your *cacerolas* [pots], not aimed at my kids or my family but at deaf ears which have failed to listen to a sector of the population which also has rights.' Marisabel, a former beauty queen, was accustomed to socialising with the very sectors of society now engaged in a life and death struggle against her husband. After three years of tightrope-walking she discovered that the middle ground had disappeared beneath her feet.[36]

## Economic downturn

The tug of war continued until February 2003, when small- and medium-sized businesses reopened their doors, admitting that the strike now threatened to turn into a 'suicide watch' that could well bankrupt their businesses for good. The strike in the oil sector dragged on for a while longer but the industry gradually regained momentum, with production levels reaching pre-strike levels by April 2003. The importation of gasoline came to an end and with it the interminable queues at petrol stations. In the meantime the government sacked about 18,000 oil workers, 40 per cent of the payroll, on the legal pretext of 'dereliction of duty', as the strikers had not walked off the job in pursuit of improved wages or labour conditions.

The collapse of the general strike marked the conclusion of a bitter 15-month period of economic and political destabilisation which reversed gains made in the first two years of the administration. The situation was bleak even before the strike began with analysts predicting a 7 per cent contraction for the year 2002. Total direct foreign investment dropped 85 per cent from $2 billion to just $456 million in the first nine months of the year. Gross domestic product shrank by 9 per cent while capital flight increased, pushing currency reserves to dangerously low levels. The Central Bank reported 3.2 per cent economic growth for the year 2000 while inflation stood at 14.2 per cent, the lowest in fifteen years. International reserves totalled $21.6 billion while the fiscal deficit dropped from 2.6 per cent of GDP in 1999 to 1.8 per cent in 2000, all of this achieved despite the emergency funds pumped into the Vargas district after the December 1999 floods.

Since then, however, the period from December 2001 to March 2003 has been characterised by a severe economic downturn. Venezuela's economy contracted by 29 per cent in the first quarter of 2003, compared with the same period the previous year. An estimated 72 per cent of households told pollsters that they have cut back on food with just half eating three meals a day. Unemployment rose to 20 per cent while the oil industry slowly returned to pre-strike production levels, with losses estimated at $10 billion. President Chávez was now faced with the urgent task of showing his supporters that his political project could deliver some of the ambitious aspirations contained in the Bolivarian constitution.

## Notes

1 *El Nacional*, June 27, 2002.
2 *The Guardian*, February 18, 2003.
3 Otto Neustadt delivered this testimony at a university seminar, 'Periodismo en tiempos de crisis', filmed in the television documentary "Anatomy of a Coup".
4 "24 Horas", Venevisión, April 12, 2002.
5 *The Financial Times*, August 22, 2002.
6 *The Guardian*, August 10, 2002.
7 'Identifican a militar estadunidense presente durante el golpe de estado contra Chávez'. *La Jornada*, April 20, 2002.
8 AFP, Reuters, April 25, 2002.
9 *El Nacional*, June 28, 2002.
10 *Extra*, April 19, 2002.
11 *El Nacional*, June 22, 2002.
12 El Universal, July 29, 2003.
13 Fair Media Advisory: 'U.S. Papers Hail Venezuelan Coup as Pro-Democracy Move', April 18, 2002.
14 'Venezuela: Caught In The Crossfire. Freedom of Expression in Venezuela', Human Rights Watch Report May 2003; 'Venezuela: Media Freedom Threatened', Human Rights Watch Press Release, February 19, 2003.
15 *La Jornada*, April 25, 2002.
16 *Notimex*, April 12, 2002.
17 *The Guardian*, April 22, 2002.
18 'Snatching defeat from the jaws of victory', Patrick Cockburn, London *Independent*, September 10, 2003.

19 *El Nacional*, June 23, 2002.

20 *El Nacional*, June 22, 2002.

21 *El Nacional*, July 11, 2002.

22 *El Nacional*, July 10, 2002.

23 *El Universal*, July 8, 2002.

24 *El Uceabista*, June–July 2002.

25 *The Guardian*, August 10, 2002.

26 *El Universal*, July 31, 2003.

27 Gott, R. 2000, *In The Shadow of the Liberator*, London: Verso, p168.

28 Letter to the *Financial Times* from Alfredo Toro Hardy, Ambassador, January 11, 2002.

29 'Defending Chavez's "Bolivarian Revolution" ', *Red Pepper*, March 13, 2003.

30 *Venezuela al Dia*, July 2001, www.venezuelaaldia.com

31 *Clarín*, November 19, 2002.

32 *The Financial Times*, October 24, 2002.

33 *Buenos Aires Herald*, December 1, 2002.

34 *The Guardian* April 11, 2003.

35 Znet commentary, April 15, 2002, www.zmag.org.

36 *El País*, December 10, 2002.

37 Ibid.

# 4
## Scenes from the
## Bolivarian Revolution

The anti-Chávez opposition groups weren't the only sectors busy taking advantage of the promises enshrined in the Bolivarian constitution. An agrarian revolution began throughout the countryside, as landless farmers seized the opportunities afforded by the land laws. Initially Article 305 of the constitution spelled out a framework for rural development:

> The state will promote sustainable agriculture as the strategic basis for integral rural development to guarantee food security, understood as the availability of sufficient foodstuffs for national consumption ... in pursuit of this goal the state will take whatever measures are necessary in terms of finance, land ownership, infrastructure, training and technology to achieve strategic levels of self-reliance.

The agrarian aspirations contained in the constitution were given practical application through 285 articles that outlined the steps required to occupy and produce on lands deemed idle or under-used after an investigation process carried out by three new land institutions. The land laws set a maximum legal size of farms, ranging from 100 to 5,000 hectares depending on productivity. A special tax was to be levied on any holding that is more than 80 per cent idle, and allowed for the redistribution of productive lands to farmers committed to their cultivation. Only high-quality idle land of over 100 hectares or lower-quality land of over 5,000 hectares can be expropriated, however, and market value must be given for it.

The Chávez administration has acknowledged that there is abundant government-owned land that can be redistributed before any private property needs to be transferred. However, landless farmers have invaded plots in a haphazard manner, desperate for a new start in life. Any Venezuelan citizen who is either the head of a family or is between 18 and 25 years old may apply for a parcel of land and, after three years of cultivation, acquire a title to it that can be passed on to descendants, but not sold. The long-term objective is to make Venezuela self-sufficient in foodstuffs by doubling GDP share in agriculture to 12 per cent by 2007. By April 2003 an estimated 200,000 hectares (500,000 acres) had been distributed to 4,500 families. That figure was set to rise to 140,000 families by the beginning of 2004, concluding the transfer of 1.5 million hectares – an average of about 10 hectares, or 25 acres, per family. The Food and Agriculture Organisation (FAO) reported that most land reforms carried out since 1945 have failed to assure either equity or efficiency because there is typically a tremendous gap between theory and practice.

The Ley de Tierras created three new institutions to back up redistribution: the National Land Institute (*Instituto Nacional de Tierras*, INTI) responsible for land tenancy; the National Rural Development Institute, (*Instituto Nacional de Desarrollo Rural*, INDR) in charge of technical and infrastructural aid to producers; and the Venezuelan Agricultural Corporation, (*Corporación Agrícola Venezolana*, CAV) to provide them with marketing assistance. The INTI began mapping the frontiers of land with *vocación agraria* (agricultural potential). The Institute would then divide land into three categories: idle, under-used or productive. The first two categories opened the door to the issuing of a *carta agraria* (agrarian deed) to landless farmers who could then legally occupy the land and receive government credit and technical assistance. Thousands of Venezuelan farmers moved onto rural land and applied for government recognition and assistance, swamping rural government offices and draining available resources. In some cases the adjudication process was hasty and ill-advised. In Zulia state 115 land titles granted by Chávez in August 2001 were declared 'irregular' by an investigating land commission and 60 were declared null and void. In Barinas state officials with the INTI discovered that land titles had been given to the wrong people, leading to a conflict between co-operatives.[1]

In the community of La Virgen, Yaracuy state, the Castaneda family has agitated for land reform for several decades as the extended family, which numbers over 100, ekes out a living on just 35 hectares of productive land. 'We have promoted a culture of *encuentros* [meetings] and personal growth,' said Gloria Castaneda, who has spent the past three decades locked in a battle for land rights. The community backed Chávez in the 1998 election campaign, anticipating speedy reform. The family formed the Union las Tres Marias co-op and secured a carta agraria, awarding an extension to their lands. But the battle was just beginning as a state governor hostile to Chávez, Eduardo Lapis, has ignored land reform decisions and sent troops to evict families occupying land across the state. 'What can you do when the revolution is proclaimed with beautiful laws but nothing happens on the ground?' asked Gloria, clearly disillusioned by the events. 'Our autonomy is being lost and there is a dangerous dependence on the government,' she added, as local Bolivarian officials urged activists to refrain from taking action that might lead to violent conflict. Several activists complained that the land struggle had become too *gobernero* – literally 'governmentalist' – as agrarian officials implementing land laws expect militants to be on their side.

The exercise of constitutional rights continues to be a risky enterprise in areas of the country under the control of anti-Chávez governors and their repressive security forces. In August 2002, in a small town in northern Venezuela, a man wearing a ski mask drove up to Pedro Doria, a respected surgeon and leader of the local land committee, called his name and, as Doria turned, shot him five times. The committee Doria led was in the process of claiming title to idle lands south of Lake Maracaibo which, according to government records, belonged to the state and could thus be legally transferred to the fifty peasant families that had applied for ownership. However, a local large landowner also claimed title to the property and on several occasions had refused to let Doria and government representatives inspect it. It is common knowledge in the region that this landowner is a close friend of former Venezuelan president Carlos Andrés Pérez, who is himself said to own over 60,000 hectares through third parties throughout the country, the vast majority of it idle. Doria was not the first peasant leader to be targeted by professional killers or para-militaries. Another who escaped from death earlier this year was José Huerta. Shot in the shoulder, he barely survived. Huerta was working for the INTI at the time and was in charge of processing the claims of Doria's committee. According to Braulio Álvarez, director of a coalition that links about a dozen peasant organisations, over fifty popular leaders have been assassinated in the past year. None of these cases has been resolved, mostly due to collusion between large landowners and the police. For example, in the cases of Doria and Huerta, the gunmen were allegedly hired by a high-ranking member of the Carlos Andrés Pérez government.

In January 2003 President Chávez attended the World Social Forum (WSF) in Porto Alegre, Brazil, the uncrowned king of the growing popular movement against corporate globalisation. The failed coup and the upper-class lockout won Chávez enormous support around the globe as activists tuned in to Chávez's diatribes against the 'new global tyranny' and marvelled at his ability to combat a powerful US-backed oligarchy. The evident support of the poor for the Chávez government confirmed the leader's position as the Fidel Castro of this era. The Cuban government has lost its lustre for many activists through its repression of non-violent dissidents. The lengthy prison sentences handed down to 28 peaceful dissidents in April 2003 marked a low point in a revolution once hailed as a symbol of global freedom. Venezuela has become an important stopoff point for global activists as José Bové, Manu Chao, Ignacio Ramonet, Eduardo Galeano, José Saramago and hundreds more public figures visiting the country in recognition of the government's attempt to redress inequalities of power and wealth. The international support movement poked fun at the absurd way the opposition stereotypes Chávez, exemplified in a remarkable Irish television documentary, *Chávez: Inside the Coup*, which won a sackful of awards and ran Michael Moore's *Bowling for Columbine* a close second as documentary of the year.

Between the two poles, however, there remained a substantial middle ground which identified with neither Chávez nor the hardline opposition. The 'ninis' (*nini* in Spanish meaning neither nor) began to gain ground, a potential bulwark in the urgent task of cooling down an over-heated political atmosphere. The opposition has alienated the 'ninis' with its blatant pursuit of the resignation of Chávez by fair means or foul, although Chávez has also failed to embrace this middle ground that will be so decisive for his government at the polls.

The OAS made an unexpected breakthrough when government officials and delegates from the Coordinadora Democrática signed a peace accord brokered by the organisation on May 19th 2003. The text of the agreement began:

> The rule of law is based on respect for the Constitution of the Bolivarian Republic of Venezuela and for the legal system that underpins it. The Constitution envisions a system of values and norms to govern fundamental principles of social and political co-existence and establishes mechanisms for reconciling differences. Any change in response to recent experiences with the political process should be based on these norms and should preferably be made through consensus.

The agreement was a modest *mea culpa* from both sides of the country's political divide but has yet to move beyond an optimistic aspiration. A previous accord, signed on February 18th 2003, the 'Declaration against Violence and for Peace and Democracy' had supposedly committed both sides to be moderate in their language and respectful in dialogue. Article 10 of the OAS agreement suggested a solution to Venezuela's permanent social violence: 'We agree to undertake a vigorous campaign to effectively disarm the civilian population.' Six months later, however, it was business as usual on Venezuela's black market for deadly weapons. Middle-class arsenals persist, and so do the traditional weapons piles in barrios where armed gangs and frightened neighbours cohabit in nervous proximity.

Meanwhile, Article 13 pledged to establish a trustworthy electoral arbiter, a goal finally achieved in August 2003, stalling future election plans. The new National Electoral Council (CNE) is accepted by both sides but faced its first vital test in the millions of signatures gathered to demand a recall referendum.

Perhaps the most crucial test of the agreement lay in Article 14, which guaranteed freedom of expression and called on the media to make citizens aware 'in an equitable and impartial manner' of their political options, to 'create a conducive climate to the successful conduct of electoral processes and referenda provided for in Article 72 of the Constitution.' Three months after the ink dried on the paper Venezuela's corporate media continued to behave like an opposition party on the campaign trail against a totalitarian tyrant, while Chávez continued to demand that the 'four horsemen of the apocalypse' (the four main TV station owners) be locked up and the keys thrown into a swamp. Still, the coming together of Venezuela's significant political currents was a modest step forward and an important reference document for monitoring both sides' behaviour in the months ahead.

## Development vs disorder: the Pemón experience

In July 2003, after an exhausting twenty-one-hour journey, I stepped gingerly off the bus into a dark night. A pinprick of light turned into an approaching cigarette held by Gregorio, my guide. He'd been waiting about six hours but didn't utter a word of reproach. More shadows appeared and we began walking in silence toward San Rafael de Kamoirán, a Pemón indigenous community close to the Venezuela–Brazil border. Out of the darkness another flickering light appeared, a single candle burning in the local church. A dog barked, a woman stirred, coffee was reheated. The bus journey had taken me from the urban jungle of Caracas to the rolling grassy highlands of the Great Savannah, a wild, vast, silent emptiness. All along the highway stood a series of huge electricity pylons, the reason for my visit.

The Pemones once roamed freely throughout the *Gran Sabana*, colonised by the Spanish then liberated by Simón Bolívar. But nothing much changed over the years no matter who was in charge; the indigenous peoples were merely ignored when they remained invisible or violently repressed if they dared defy development plans. On the campaign trail in 1998, Hugo Chávez promised to revise the constitution and insert a new charter of indigenous rights. He also promised to suspend and review an electricity project which carved an unwanted path through Pemón territory. The electricity project involved 676 kilometres of high tension cable stretching from Venezuela into Roraima state in Brazil. Similar development projects in nearby states had led to encroachment by mining and tourism, creating havoc among the communities.

The Pemones lead quiet lives, relying on their *conuco*, a small plot of land where yucca, bananas and corn are grown. The Pemones backed Chávez and participated in the drafting of the articles of the Bolivarian constitution which recognised the indigenous as the first peoples of Venezuela – a remarkable leap forward. The constitution also pledged to demarcate all indigenous territory within two years, although the final wording disappointed activists when the concept of 'territory' was replaced by 'habitat'.

Silviano Castro, a Pemón leader, organised busloads of Pemón families to visit Caracas and defend the government project, which came under fire from big business and the Catholic Church. Silviano, a short, heavy-set man in his mid-thirties, was the community capitán, or leader, throughout the process. 'All we asked was that the project be suspended so that a proper study of the impact could be made,' Silviano said as we shared a plate of rice and boiled insects.

Once the constitution was approved, the pressure began. If the Pemones wanted to secure their rights they had to support the electricity project which would bring in the millions of dollars required to turn the Bolivarian dream into reality. The Pemón communities, scattered across the border zone, were divided on the issue, as most communities accepted government promises of money and food in return for project support. While on the campaign trail Chávez had said that if gold were discovered in the Amazon he would prefer to leave it buried there rather than damage the indigenous communities of the vicinity. Once in office President Chávez announced a consultation plan to placate indigenous and environmental concerns. Government delegates arrived with a clipboard and a questionnaire, treating the process as a necessary formality toward a foregone conclusion. This consultation plan failed to satisfy a number of Pemón communities who understood 'consultation' to be a detailed series of discussions, the outcome of which was uncertain but mutually determined. President Chávez ordered the completion of the project despite the strenuous objections of ten Pemón communities, including San Rafael de Kamoiran. Maria, an elderly Pemón, gave me her opinion on development: 'development is something that happens inside each man and woman, it is the wisdom learned from nature as we work our lands…. For you outsiders development means material things … you spend your time locked up in your homes … we don't call that development.'

San Rafael de Kamoiran stood firm, and when the bulldozers restarted work the new pylons began to fall in the dead of night. The harassment began after an Army general turned up at San Rafael on December 26th offering food parcels to each family but was turned away. The visiting General claimed there was no connection between the food handouts and the pylon campaign but the community feared that by accepting the food offer they somehow legitimised the army presence on their lands. The army soldiers told locals that they were frontier guards on routine patrol in the area but one Pemón soldier, speaking the language of the local people, admitted that they had orders 'to grab the Indians who were felling the pylons.'

On December 27th 2000 a group of about 40 masked men surrounded Silviano's home then withdrew. The following night they returned, this time without masks. The soldiers returned at one in the morning the following day in vehicles belonging to the pylon construction company. One San Rafael youth, 22-year-old Juan Ramón Lezama, disappeared. He stumbled home the next day, covered in bruises after two soldiers forced him into one of their vehicles and took him to a nearby camp. The community logged several violations of the Bolivarian constitution, notably Article 46 which safeguards the right to 'physical integrity', while the entire community repudiated the violation of their right to 'psychic and moral integrity' due to the late-night harassment by the army patrols. The army had also interrogated villagers and taken working tools away from them, thus violating the right to property as enshrined in Article 115, and the right to free transit (Article 50) when they ordered locals to return to their homes at night. The army operation also violated the community's right as indigenous citizens (Articles 119 and 121) which decrees respect for the culture, security and daily life of the nation's first inhabitants. Army camps were set up beside indigenous communities, activists were harassed and when indigenous families ordered the soldiers out of their communities they were met with tear gas and rubber bullets. Finally, in May 2002 Miguel Lanz, a Pemón aged 25, was shot dead in cold blood by an army soldier in front of five witnesses. No-one was punished and the community retreated, unwilling to risk more bloodshed. The battle was over.

The electricity pylon project signed by Rafael Caldera and Fernando Henrique Cardoso in 1997 was finally inaugurated in August 2002 when Cardoso and Chávez were joined by Fidel Castro to celebrate a victory for progress. Insult was piled on injury when it was revealed that the original plan to supply electricity all the way to Manaus in Brazil had been cancelled. The vast project is currently only feeding electricity to two small border towns, one in Brazil and one in Venezuela. The Pemón experience offered a sobering reminder that regardless of the supposed protection of a progressive constitution, indigenous peoples remain pawns in the development game.

---

## In the ghetto/Chapellines

'In the church everyone is an activist, not just members of an illuminated left-wing sect,' said Father Juan Vives, a Salesian priest of Spanish origin. Vives, like many church radicals, supports Chávez but remains aloof from Bolivarian institutions. 'We are transforming negative bitterness and sadness into a creative, transforming and positive energy.' The wiry, energetic 80-year-old was addressing neighbours in the working-class Chapellines barrio, a crazy legoland of passageways leading to precarious homes stacked layer upon layer like baked beans in a supermarket. It was Sunday afternoon, there was noise and bustle, children and grandparents, bicycles and balconies with Brazilian flags draped on windows in honour of the recent World Cup victory (this was June

2002). Almost on cue, a barrio activist joined in with a football metaphor: 'Over time the coup will be seen as an own goal which eliminated the opposition from the competition,' said Victor Belis, a community organiser involved with a local urban land committee.

Speeches and games were being held to celebrate the formal handover of property titles to the urban squatters. The Chapellines community groups have replaced clientelism with co-responsibility, a term now tripping from the tongues of ordinary citizens. 'We get a budget, we organise the projects, we evaluate, we control, not central government,' concluded Belis. Respect for the church presence was evident as Father Vives was greeted like a popstar, despite his unassuming manner. 'God is here,' one woman told him. 'This is organised love,' she added, once more shattering the illusion of godless communism infiltrating the hearts and minds of the people. The handover of property titles was followed by an afternoon of poetry and drama with contemporary dance, traditional music, comedians and, to conclude, a martial arts display with what looked like medieval Japanese weaponry. 'We must train because the *escualidos* [the squalid ones, echoing Chávez' indictment of the oligarchy] are also training,' said the local karate champion.

Over the past fifty years the state has built one million homes and the private sector twice that figure while the residents of impoverished barrios, who have infinitely fewer resources, have built over three million. It has been suggested that upwards of ten million Venezuelans may benefit from the urban property transfer deal, some 40 per cent of the population. Iván Martínez, the director of the National Technical Office for the Regularization of Urban Land Tenancy, described the urban citizenship programme as 'a recognition of the social debt which the state owes the population.' Andrés Antillano, a housing activist who worked with Martínez on the draft of the urban property law, added that the aim of the project was to 'recognise the barrio as a collective subject with legal rights and profound transformative potentials.'

Peruvian economist Hernando de Soto, a neo-liberal guru who believes that all human beings are born for the sole purpose of engaging in commercial transactions, has identified urban squatters as the key to unlocking vast amounts of untapped capital. De Soto recommends that urban land titles be awarded to squatters so that the impoverished residents can mortgage their homes to obtain business credit. In contrast, Chávez's supporters view the process as a crucial step toward participatory democracy and community autonomy.

## PDVSA

The oil strike gave Chávez the golden opportunity of sacking half the PDVSA workforce without falling foul of the country's stringent labour laws. The opposition described the restructuring of the oil sector as the 'destruction' of PDVSA, insisting that the consequences of massive dismissals will necessarily be catastrophic at a technical level. It is still too soon to tell what the long-term impact on the oil industry will be, but a year after the April 2002 coup Chávez had brought the country's two most powerful institutions, the army and PDVSA, firmly under government control.

In a deal cut between the Ministry of Energy and Mines and US-based Free Market Petroleum LLC in January 2003, the Chávez administration agreed to supply the US strategic petroleum reserve at the rate of 50,000 barrels a day for an initial three-year period. The sale was confirmed precisely as the oil strike reached a turning point at home and marked the end of US support for the Venezuelan right-wing oil opposition. Left-wing critics denounced the manoeuvre as a sell-out to the evil empire, but in the critical juncture of the two-month general strike and in the face of virtual economic collapse, Chávez swallowed his pride and temporarily neutralised one of his key opponents.

The high stakes chess game continued. In response the US Government muted its criticism of Chávez. By July 2003 the opposition was murmuring that US ambassador Charles Shapiro was being too 'soft' on Chávez. But it appeared Shapiro was merely playing the diplomatic game: a short time before, Ambassador Shapiro had invited the opposition to his residence on International Freedom Day (May 21ˢᵗ) where a comedian performed a crude sketch based on President Chávez. In response, an assembly of middle-class Chavistas, the *Foro de Constitución y Paz*, held a discussion on how best to upbraid the ambassador. It was decided to send him copies of the US and Venezuelan constitutions, along with various international accords detailing the remit of foreign diplomats. Within three hours of the dispatch of the package Shapiro apologised profusely, and in a surprise move the US ambassador acknowledged the 'free and participatory' nature of the Venezuelan political system. Ambassador Shapiro sought unsuccessfully to revoke the US visa of Carlos Andrés Pérez for commenting publicly that Chávez's departure from office would only occur through violence. He also successfully lobbied to revoke the US visa of a former Venezuelan army general Enrique Medina Gómez, a prominent critic of Chávez. The visa was cancelled on the grounds that Medina has connections to 'terrorism', even though the dissident general has not formally been accused of terror offences under Venezuelan law. Medina, a former military attaché in Washington, maintained close ties with Otto Reich, the White House's special envoy for Latin America.[2] At the time of writing, (November 2003) US Government officials have launched a fresh offensive against President Chávez, claiming that Islamic terror units are training in Venezuela. The Venezuelan government responded with accusations that hardline opposition activists were meeting CIA operatives to plan an assassination attempt on Chávez. There was no hard evidence offered in either case.

## Foro Constitución y Paz

The Peace and Constitutional Forum, *Foro Constitución y Paz*, a middle-class gathering based in the Chacao district, has held several citizen assemblies to debate issues of public relevance in which anyone can speak. The group held one such meeting to discuss the future of PDVSA and debate reforms in the oil sector. Some 500 people attended the assembly and the resulting document was handed in to the president of PDVSA, who then invited a Foro delegation to discuss the document in his office. The Foro delegates refused the offer, insisting instead that PDVSA chiefs attend one of their weekly assemblies and address the entire forum. The same Foro group has held several assemblies outside corporate media offices, complaining of the biased coverage of current events. The Foro takes its job seriously, bringing its own chairs and tables; minutes are taken and a public notary employed to verify the decisions taken by the collective. Not to be outdone, the opposition has organised dozens of assemblies, but there is no spontaneous debate, just a roll call of predetermined speakers spanning the usual reduced spectrum of virulent anti-Chávez opinion.

Meanwhile the 'new' PDVSA has begun to take shape under the influence of Rafael Ramírez, the Minister of Energy and Mines. Ramirez announced a fresh round of spending cuts in July 2003 'due to the reduced workforce and their bonuses, salaries and privileges.'[3] The sacking of thousands of oil workers was a complicated matter, as many employees had been given homes close to oil production centres that they refused to abandon. Government supporters, who had set up tent cities outside oil installations to guard against sabotage during the strike, now turned their attention to ousting the oil workers from their homes. Violence flared in Zulia state as Chávez supporters faced down former oil workers while National Guard troops intervened with tear gas to break up the disturbances. In one night of violence 26 people were injured in Lagunillas.[4]

The situation was further complicated by the presence of an estimated 3,000 schoolchildren who will not be eligible to return to classes. Ali Rodríguez, president of PDVSA, visited the zone and announced plans to forcibly eject former workers from the oil camps.

> These workers abandoned the company of their own free will. The labour relationship is over, they no longer enjoy the contractual benefits they had within the company. We were decent enough to let the children finish off their school year and we will now follow all the required legal steps so that they abandon the area and with it, all the benefits to which they were entitled.[5]

Meanwhile, the departure of the oil executives created a well-heeled diaspora as they moved on to fresh pastures in Canada and the US, but not before venting their bitterness against Venezuelans for failing to oust Chávez. In one testimony, a former PDVSA executive Jorge Robles outlined his reasons for downing tools: 'The country I wanted for myself and my family was no longer possible under this regime, so I couldn't continue working in my office.' En route to Canada, Robles blamed the failure of the general strike on citizens whose only participation in events was 'to press the remote control to see what was happening on Globovision.' In a symbolic move Chávez appropriated several PDVSA buildings to house the first Bolivarian University, formally opened in July 2003, even though courses, professors and students had yet to be organised. Chávez promised that 400,000 students who failed to find a place in third-level education would eventually be accommodated in the new educational establishment.

On the economic front, the nation's currency reserves stabilised after Chávez introduced currency controls in February 2003 to combat speculation and punish the business class for the general strike. The currency control scheme deprived businesses of the dollars required to engage in international business deals. Chávez announced that there would be no dollars for coup plotters. By June 2003 the government had approved the sale of just $100 million, a sum that would be demanded by business every three days in normal times. The currency restrictions hurt big business but also led to thousands of job losses as manufacturing companies laid off workers in the absence of dollar transactions. On the black market the dollar cost 50 per cent more than the official rate.[6] Politically, President Chávez suffered the abdication of allies at this time, and growing dissension among the ranks of his own movement as his parliamentary majority was shaved to a bare three-seat advantage.

## National Union of Workers

In August 2003, Venezuela's National Union of Workers (*Unión Nacional de Trabajadores*, UNT) held its first National Congress to determine the ground rules for a new workers' federation, discussing internal statutes, election mechanisms, code of ethics, basic principles and action programme. The final outcome was a call for further debate and consultation with each individual union. The UNT was founded in April 2003 to provide a voice and instrument for working people opposed to the anti-Chávez bias of the CTV.

This first Congress brought together more than 1300 registered participants representing 120 unions and 25 regional federations. Participants called for the transformation of 'capitalist society into a self-managing society,' for a 'new model of anti-capitalist and autonomous development that emancipates human beings from class exploitation, oppression, discrimination and exclusion.' The delegates declared support for the Chávez administration but criticised specific government ministries, demanding that unpopular labour inspectors be removed by the labour ministry and that a national emergency be declared by the health ministry. The debate was open and heated with some delegates claiming that proposed UNT statutes were far too like those of the

CTV, an organisation infamous for its lack of internal democracy and for its corruption. Most of the unions represented at the gathering had left the CTV in opposition to its alliance with employers' federation Fedecamaras during the coup and general strike. The debate on recall procedures, term limits, asset declarations, proportional representation and distribution of dues reached an unexpected conclusion: to go back to the base and consult each individual union for a full discussion of the issues.

There was disagreement too when the UNT's temporary 21-member steering committee decided that the Unitary Confederation of Workers (*Confederación Unitaria de Trabajadores Venezolanos*, CUTV), an affiliate of the World Federation of Trade Unions, which had been involved in the creation of UNT from the outset, could not integrate with its regional organisations; as a result many of its militants stayed away from this congress. One conspicuous absence from the gathering was Ramón Machuca, influential leader of the Steelworkers Union, who had departed from early UNT discussions, citing the need for more initial work at the base and the creation of worker constituent assemblies around the country. The most conspicuous absence was that of Chávez himself, who was invited to close the Congress. Not only did he not appear, but neither the vice-president nor the Minister of Labour came to take his place. On 'Aló Presidente' the next day Chávez made a point of congratulating Machuca ('a friend') on his re-election as Steelworker leader (he gained 63 per cent of the votes against a strong right-wing challenge).

The new union will have a tough task ahead if it hopes to enjoy official favour and steer an independent line on behalf of its members. In an attempt to broaden its support base and adapt to changing labour conditions, the UNT emphasised the need to create committees of the unemployed and for food stamps to buy food for pensioners and the jobless. The UNT has yet to establish its relationship with workers in the informal sector, a vital link to more than 50 per cent of Venezuela's twelve million strong workforce.

On August 19th 2003 Chávez reached the halfway point in his administration. The opposition marked the occasion by handing him an estimated 2.7 million signatures demanding a recall referendum. Undeterred by the defeat of the coup and the collapse of the general strike, the opposition pinned their hopes on the Bolivarian constitution, once more taking advantage of its liberal provisions. The first decision of the new Electoral Council was to annul the signatures collected by the opposition in February, saying that the opposition had failed to observe the required guidelines. Mid-term elections were set for June 4th 2004, in which mayors, governors and local officials would face a popular ballot – a crucial test of Chávez's durability. The National Electoral Council also ruled that upcoming gubernatorial and congressional elections be held over two weekends (June 20th and 27th 2004) while the contest for mayoral and local government posts will be held in December of that year.

## Help, help the Commies are coming! (July 2003)

Venezuela's opposition media alerted the nation about an imminent 'communist invasion' in June 2003 when Cuban doctors and teachers arrived in the country to spearhead literacy and preventive health programmes in impoverished neighbourhoods. One newspaper speculated that the Cubans were Angolan combat veterans in disguise come to fight alongside Chávez should he be ousted from power, while another radio station assured listeners that Chávez had printed a million passports for Cuban immigrants who would then vote for their benefactor in a possible mid-term recall referendum, evoking echoes of the Pérez Jiménez era when privileged European immigrants were speedily 'nationalised' to allow them vote on behalf of the dictator in a plebiscite on his continued rule.

On board a bus one day I overheard one woman tell the passenger beside her that the doctors were actually veterinarians and were busy killing off the natives with liberal prescriptions of horse tranquillisers. The media also claimed that the Cubans were indoctrinating patients at their clinics, presumably brandishing antibiotics in one hand, a volume of *Das Kapital* in the other. The only Venezuelans who didn't seem to mind the 'invasion' were the poor citizens living in shacks on the hillsides of Caracas who were enjoying the company of a trained doctor living in their communities for the first time. Cuba has also given advanced medical treatment to 4,000 Venezuelan patients in Havana free of charge while 557 students are studying at Cuba's Latin American School of Medicine and will replace the Cuban doctors when they complete their medical training.

When I visited the San José neighbourhood in June 2003, Nirvando Pérez was busy attending a queue of women holding feverish children while several elderly men coughed in the background. Pérez is one of 1,000 Cuban doctors who have come to Venezuela to work on Barrio Adentro, 'Inside the Neighbourhood', a plan aimed at providing preventive health care to one million Venezuelans living in underprivileged areas. In the tiny clinic which accommodated a bed, a small desk and three people, a woman explained how the pills she had been given for insomnia no longer worked and that she was driven mad at night. Dr Pérez asked her questions about her lifestyle, ferreting out details of stress and marital separation, then suggested the woman stay off the pills and consult a psychiatrist instead. The young Cuban doctor held a morning clinic, then visited homes in the afternoon and was on call 24 hours a day. In the two months since he had come to Venezuela he had had just one day off. He missed his family back in Santiago de Cuba and privately expressed his wish to be home by Christmas. A fanatical reader, Nirvando told me he had devoured 1,200 biographies and was currently chomping through a life of Simón Bolívar lent to him by a neighbour.

On a stroll through the network of narrow streets outside the makeshift clinic, Pérez gestured at rubbish left uncollected outside homes and explained that the main focus of the health mission was to impress upon neighbours the need to establish a clean, healthy environment as a first step toward reducing related illnesses.

Cuban doctors are respected whereever they work, from Guatemala to South Africa, under right- and left-wing regimes, going where local doctors refuse to go. 'The Venezuelan doctor expects a big salary,' Health Minister Maria Urbaneja told me. 'They have no interest in working in a poor neighbourhood for a pittance.' The Caracas city authorities responsible for the plan first advertised for Venezuelan doctors in a daily newspaper, seeking professionals willing to work for low pay in under-privileged areas of the city. The response was paltry – a couple of dozen inquiries that fell far short of the ambitious government plan. The conditions were far too chaotic for most Venezuelan professionals, who expect to hold clinics at fixed hours. The advertisement required doctors to live in the neighbourhood and be available day and night for emergency cases, all for less than $200 a month. 'Working for the city council,' conceded one newspaper columnist, 'is worse than being unemployed.'[8] It was then that President Chávez turned to Cuba, which has a considerable surplus of doctors imbued with a commitment to popular health care.

As hundreds of doctors arrived in Caracas, a smaller group of Cubans disembarked to lead a literacy campaign aimed at reaching over one million citizens. The Cuba-sponsored literacy programme, 'Plan Robinson' (a pseudonym used by Bolívar's mentor Simón Rodríguez), strongly recommended by UNESCO, once more ignited the ire of the opposition, who claimed the visitors intended to indoctrinate their pupils. The three-month literacy programme is based around family ties and popular games. There are just 74 Cuban technical advisors who monitor the progress of 50,000 Venezuelan literacy volunteers. Cuban President Fidel Castro not only offered the instruction videos free of charge – he also presented the

Venezuelan government with 50,000 Chinese television sets and video recorders required for the programme.

The health-care and literacy projects offer nothing to the middle classes, who enjoy the benefits of private health programmes and university education. Cuban doctors have come under attack from organised opposition groups in some neighbourhoods but there have only been minor skirmishes to date. 'We must organise, leave our fear behind and boot the Cubans out of the barrios, schools and hospitals to show Chávez that we don't want them here,' said Haydee Deutsh, a leader of Fuerza Liberal and a founder member of the umbrella opposition alliance Coordinadora Democrática.[9] Venezuela's corporate media launched a vicious campaign against the Cubans, spreading lies, rumour and gossip to undermine popular confidence in the project. The verbal hate campaign turned nasty when a molotov cocktail destroyed a mobile health clinic used by the Barrio Adentro campaign.[10] Newspapers run front-page tales of alleged medical malpractice by Cuban doctors on a daily basis, a litany of lies that goes completely unchecked.

'Every education system has an ideological bias,' explained Roberto Flores, an education official defending the literacy programme, 'but up until now it has been the church and the upper classes who have dictated the nature of the bias.'

Josefina Montiel, taking her first steps toward writing her name thanks to the literacy campaign, summed up the mood among those putting pen to paper for the first time: 'I want to be the person I'm not,' she said, proudly taking hold of her pen. Just as Venezuela, on a larger scale, aspires to be the country it yet isn't – healthy, educated and independent.

## Movimiento V República

The Movimiento Quinta República (MVR) consists of all the different political sectors that lend support to Hugo Chávez's political leadership, but is dominated by veterans of the left-wing movements that have ebbed and flowed across the political landscape over the past forty years. The *Patria Para Todos*, *Liga Socialista* and *Movimiento Electoral del Pueblo* are all expressions of the 'revolutionary democratic left', while the Bolivarian Circles provide a loose-knit support structure for Chávez in the neighbourhoods.

But the organic link between Chávez and the masses is formed by the card-carrying Bolivarian activists gathered into the *Círculos Patrióticos* or Patriotic Circles. These Circles are divided into national, regional, municipal and parish command centres which elect sixty delegates to a National Strategic Directorate that in turn elects a 30-member National Tactical Command, the equivalent of an MVR cabinet. The executive body includes prominent public figures like parliamentary deputies Adan Chávez (brother of Hugo), Iris Varela and Juan Barreto, alongside Freddy Bernal, mayor of Libertador district, as well as some lesser-known faces. 'Our aim is to win over fifteen to twenty per cent of the population which is wavering in its political position,' said Augusto Montiel, a public management expert and university professor elected to the MVR's National Directorate in June 2003. Some 800,000 members of the Patriotic Circles participated in these elections. President Chávez is anxious to organise a national movement to defend his government as a recall referendum appears likely for 2004. The government's parliamentary majority has shrunk to a narrow margin, sustained by 83 'solid votes' and a handful of floating legislators from *Podemos* and *Vamos*, splinter groups that broke with the MAS leadership and formed independent parliamentary groups. The opposition, meanwhile, has 79 seats.

The Chavista movement is hampered by its struggle to reconcile its populist short-term appeal with the need to institutionalise the Bolivarian project. Chávez unveils a new financial assistance package almost every weekend on 'Aló Presidente', offering all school leavers a place in university, along with US$100 welfare grants for low-income families. The literacy programme is driven by its participants' hopes that loyalty to the scheme will guarantee a small credit while many community groups register themselves as Bolivarian Circles in the hope that economic assistance will follow. Unless Chávez can lay down deeper roots in the population, however, his populist appeal will last only as long as competitive oil revenues flow into state coffers.

The debate on reform and revolution has accompanied the Venezuelan government ever since Hugo Chávez assumed office, winning through peaceful means what he failed to achieve with a military uprising. Chávez sympathisers have debated the issue of power with the Zapatista movement in southeast Mexico, where indigenous rebels have rejected the presidential throne as an empty vessel. The struggle for power, the Zapatistas say, is a losing battle in which the alternative project is swallowed up by bureaucracy and corporate hostility. The task is to dissolve power itself and build an autonomous alternative through collective action.

President Chávez assumed office on a wave of popular support, but has seen his energy and optimism eroded in the continuous war waged by corporations, the oil industry, the mainstream media and the upper class. 'Manipulation and manoeuvring for power become a way of life,' cautioned John Holloway in his influential book *Change the World Without Taking Power*. Social relations in Venezuela are undergoing fundamental changes as the dispossessed majority enjoy modest improvements to their lives. However, the survival of the Chávez administration has become a percentage game as activists calculate the required number of votes to maintain power. Internal competition for MVR posts has resulted in fisticuffs as candidates compete for selection in upcoming election battles. A friend in the Foreign Ministry told me how fellow workers danced on the tables when the President announced (on 'Aló Presidente') that a two million Bolívar ($2,000) bonus would be paid to public employees before

Christmas 2003. 'Chávez is obviously planning to hold the referendum,' was the conclusion. There is no doubt that the urban land titles, agrarian reform, literacy programme, state-run basic food distribution networks, Saraos, urban gardens and other projects all contribute to empowering the dispossessed majority. But the vast majority of Venezuelan citizens remain bystanders to the political process, waiting for results to be delivered, like the two million Bolivares promised to public service workers. The windfall oil revenues continue to power the political system, and financial largesse underpins loyalty to the government of the day.

## By way of a conclusion

'This revolution is peaceful but it is not unarmed.'
Hugo Chávez, speaking at the World Social Forum, January 2003.

Fidel Castro has been an important source of wisdom for the impulsive Venezuelan president, never more so than during the April 2002 coup. That afternoon the beleaguered Chávez placed an emergency call to Havana: '*no te vayas a inmolar,*' Castro told Chávez – 'Don't go out in a blaze of glory.' Chávez was inside the presidential palace, threatened with aerial bombardment by dissident troops, just as Salvador Allende had been when General Augusto Pinochet ousted the democratic socialist in September 1973. '*Eres un hombre joven, no haces lo de Allende, cuida la vida de los hombres.*' 'You're a young man,' Castro said, 'don't do an Allende on it, honour life.'

Despite the fiery rhetoric and his previous career as a coup plotter, Hugo Chávez has no appetite for violence. Chávez's comment at the WSF that opens this section points to his leniency toward the opposition ranged against him, and serves as a reminder that there was more backing his project that his own will. Meanwhile the opposition, lacking a credible leader or an alternative political project, relies on the threat of force to advance its agenda. 'Those who protest are not hungry, not homeless, not unemployed and not landless,' said Chávez, accurately defining the nature of the more radical opposition elements.

There is a general assumption that when a candidate wins election to presidential office in Latin America they immediately take control of what Douglas Bravo calls the 'real elements of power', meaning industry, the media, security forces and other crucial power levers. In fact the triumphant victor generally secures only a quota of power, conditional on the backing of the military, business, church and media, not forgetting the enormous influence of US foreign policy pressures. The Punto Fijo parties, AD and COPEI, successfully hitched their political bandwagons to the country's traditional power brokers. The arbitrary nature of the Pérez Jiménez regime convinced the elite that more complex social and political machinery were required to dominate the masses and ensure widespread support for (or resignation towards) its conservative agenda.

President Chávez has attempted to bypass the political machinery and dominate the power brokers through an alliance of informal traders, landless farmers, small businesses, students and retired citizens, establishing a loyal chain extending upwards toward the hillside barrios. The middle and upper classes fear that the hillsides will descend to loot and plunder their wealth – a factor that is both a deterrent and a spur to ousting Chávez. If Chávez remains in office, social unrest may be contained; yet if Chávez continues to stoke the flames of class warfare, the long-term threat to wealth and privilege may be even greater. President Chávez's ability to deliver short-term gains to his loose coalition of supporters will determine his political survival.

In Venezuela today the US imperial agenda, the corporate media and the Catholic Church hierarchy are powerful opposition blocs to Chávez. The army and the oil sector have been neutralised, but further obstacles lie ahead. Chávez's strength lies in his ability to mobilise the grassroots behind his project but time is scarce as economic downturn tests the patience of the poor. The task before Chávez is a herculean one, admitted Michael Nylin, president of General Motors in Venezuela. 'If the only task facing Chávez was that of building a new country that would be work enough for two lifetimes, but Señor Chávez has a tougher task than that; he must put order in the institutions and in all aspects of society to change people's attitudes.'

President Chávez's favourite anniversary is undoubtedly the one known as F-4, the anniversary of his failed coup attempt on February 4th 1992. While Chávez has been successful in revamping the nation's institutions, his democratic, electoral mandate has limited his ability to purge key institutions that maintain strong links to the past. No doubt he envies Fidel Castro, who came to power with absolute authority and dissolved the security forces, rebuilding them in his image. The nation's police force is of doubtful loyalty, particularly officers responding to anti-Chávez mayors and governors who have repressed pro-Chávez gatherings. In addition Chávez has been forced to treat an aggressive, provocative media with kid gloves, undermining his efforts to build Bolivarian consciousness through the mass media.

One has only to look at the behaviour of the media in the US to see just how frustrating the situation is for Chávez. During the invasion of Iraq dissent was dismissed as unpatriotic and the media rowed in unquestioningly behind Bush's war of aggression, meekly accepting their role as cheerleaders for the military effort. The atmosphere in the US was tense as citizens competed with each other to demonstrate their pro-war credentials. In middle-class Caracas the mood is similar, as apartment block residents tolerate no shows of support for Chávez, with verbal aggression and threats the order of the day. As I walked through the Parque del Este, located in a wealthy suburb, school kids aged eight were chanting 'Death to Chávez', their bemused teachers feigning surprise at the outburst. Teachers are by no means neutral figures in the conflict – private schools used school buses to ferry teachers to anti-Chávez marches while one teacher faced charges of incitement to hatred after urging the overthrow of Chávez at a parent–teacher meeting.

Hugo Chávez's power plans shifted after 1992 when his failed military rebellion evolved into an electoral project aimed at implementing peaceful, democratic reforms. President Chávez's revolutionary dreams have since been downsized to the point where the best-case scenario is the insertion of Venezuela into the globalised economic arena on more favourable terms than might have occurred under a neo-liberal administration. In other words – a kinder, gentler version of the corporate global agenda. President Chávez's rejection of the FTAA, his call for a multipolar global order and his ongoing reform project represent minor alterations in power structures, particularly when key allies in Brazil and Ecuador have narrowed their focus to winning consensus for anti-poverty programmes.

Meanwhile the US military machine patrols the globe in search of dissident nations that might require a little pre-emptive discipline to remind them who rules the world. Venezuela under Chávez is a prime target for the US war machine, and neighbouring Colombia remains embroiled in a chronic internal conflict in which the US government is taking a far more active role than ever before. Historically, US intervention in Latin America has been designed to improve the investment climate for corporate business interests. Plan Colombia has been a runaway success as private US companies win lucrative security contracts, while President Álvaro Uribe has turned his back on regional allies to negotiate a bilateral trade agreement with the US. Venezuela's alternative perspective on globalisation remains an obstacle to the corporate steam-roller as it rides through the region. Elias Santana, a prominent opposition leader, succinctly described what is at stake: 'The way in which Chávez is ousted will define the future path of Venezuela'.[11]

In early 2004 Chávez and Lula will conclude the first phase of a regional economic integration plan linking the Andean nations (Bolivia, Colombia, Ecuador, Venezuela and Peru) with Mercosur (Argentina, Brazil, Paraguay and Uruguay) and the Caribbean into a powerful trade bloc. Venezuelan political analyst Alberto Garrido believes that Chávez may have a second wind: 'The opposition rushed into the coup because they know it will be too late in a year or two,' Garrido told me. 'Chávez is putting down roots and interfering with the pillars of society which were believed to be untouchable.' Garrido concluded, somewhat philosophically, that 'Venezuelans have no one to represent them, no one who speaks to them, no singers, no unions, no political parties, so they have turned Chávez into a myth.'[12]

The collapse of the welfare state and the opening of the economy toward speculative rather than productive capital has consolidated two Venezuelas, separated not just by barbed wire and police guns but by radically divergent visions of citizenship and personal destiny. One Venezuela is an internationally connected business class and its local associates, controlling significant sectors of the economy. The second Venezuela lives in the hillsides and survives on its wits, in constant search of a messiah with a magical formula to relieve them of their misery. As we know, the messiah strategy is a recipe for futile martyrdom. One Chávez supporter interviewed on television made the following observation which was immediately adopted as a Bolivarian slogan: '*Con hambre y sin empleo con Chávez me resteo*,' which means 'Hungry and unemployed I'm sticking with Chávez all the way.' The comment came in the context of the deteriorating economic situation that followed the general strike in February 2003. The hopeless rallying cry struck me as a negative and depressing reminder that an element of hardline

Chavismo, just like the hardline opposition ranged against it, would sooner see the country sink into the sea rather than hand over power. Chávez supporters disagreed with this pessimistic interpretation, insisting that the slogan demonstrated 'the hope and awareness' generated by the Chávez administration.

Chávez has the halo of martyrdom around him, the indelible mark of someone who risked his life to change the unjust economic order, an important factor in a nation where ordinary people risk their lives simply returning home from work along unsafe streets each evening. That halo shone brighter for his supporters after the failed April 2002 coup as Chávez once more demonstrated remarkable calm in the face of mortal danger, refusing to give in even when the odds seemed irrevocably stacked against him. The collapse of the general strike has heightened this sense of invincibility. Meanwhile the opposition blame Chávez for everything, to the degree that one newspaper attributed an epidemic of 'muscular spasms, gastritis, irritable colon and tooth fractures' to the stress of life under Chávez. A recent poll of polls cross-referenced dozens of studies to gauge the popular mood. The results showed that Chávez's support ranged from between 30 per cent and 44 per cent in the eighteen months following the April 2002 coup. Support was highest at times of extreme tension with 44 per cent backing the leader after the April 2002 coup while 37 per cent declared support after the general strike in March 2003. Chávez thrives on adversity while the opposition continue to strike below the belt, alienating ordinary Venezuelans. Chávez enjoys support among the informal sector, some five million self-employed street sellers and suppliers who constitute 52 per cent of the working population. Although he initially reduced unemployment from 18 to 13 per cent, figures shot up 20 per cent after the crippling strike and are now hovering at 18 per cent, although these figures also have to be examined in a regional context – nearby Colombia suffers 20 per cent unemployment, Argentina 25 per cent.

When it comes to analysing the Hugo Chávez phenomenon, observers have quoted Marx, Mao and Fidel Castro, but the real Chávez – if such a thing exists – is to be found in astrological circles. When you switch on early morning television or radio in Venezuela, the chances are you will be deluged by astrological charts, psychics and tarot card readers, all offering horoscopes and predictions in an effort to make sense of the chaos around them. Shortly after the April 2002 coup attempt I bumped into an aunt of Chávez's at a neighbourhood fiesta. 'God put him there in the first place,' she said, 'so God had to rescue him and bring him back.'

Chávez is a remarkable exception to the norm in a political universe where consent is manufactured through spin, lies and the use of overwhelming force. An old woman described the phenomenon: 'For me, it is as if my own son was president,' she said, accurately describing the feeling that comes across from this man of the people. A friend of mine who dislikes Chávez's politics told me that she had to stop listening to him because every time she heard him she fell under the spell and forgot why she opposed him. A small example of Chávez in action on "Aló Presidente" reveals his folksy style which links class warfare with garlic sauce:

> Yesterday I left Miraflores at three in the morning and stopped to buy a hot dog and I remembered a book I'd read a short while ago. The hot dog was damn good, I really like them with garlic sauce, it reminds me of when I was a kid in Sabaneta, no one could make a garlic sauce like my grandmother, nobody, anyway the book described how the upper classes always lived the Country Club lifestyle, locked away and never caring what happened to the people living on the other side of the fence, hey you (pointing to a woman in the audience) how do you make garlic sauce?'

It is hard to imagine another politician anywhere in the world who could pull off such esoteric oratory.

On the international stage, the Chávez administration continues to forge an independent path, rejecting the Cancún round of trade talks in September 2003 with the comment that 'Venezuela recognises the supremacy of international accords in the area of human rights, health, food security and biodiversity above the intellectual property rights of transnational corporations.'

President Chávez, the 'flawed idealist' and 'democrat in a hurry' continues to fight for a more just economic system. But after five years in power Chávez has failed to reform or rethink the nature of power itself. Perhaps the best thing that Chávez could do would be to retire from power, even if he survives the recall referendum test. In July 2004 Hugo Chávez will turn fifty years of age, a useful vantage point to view the future ahead. In political terms he is still a young man. Chávez revamped state institutions while also attempting to alter deeply rooted social relationships in a divided and frightened society.

Nor does the opposition present a credible alternative. If Hugo Chávez were to be removed from the political landscape the ensuing scramble for power would reduce the opposition unity to an ugly scrum. The Coordinadora Democrática consists of 19 political parties spanning the ideological spectrum yet it lacks even a hint of how to build a political project and is united only by the goal of ousting Chávez. The likelihood is that a non-Chávez government would attempt to impose the neo-liberal project on a people who, through the Chávez experiment, have gained enormous awareness of their own power. Will such a government accept the challenge of a recall referendum halfway through its own term of office? Which presidential candidate will dare to go to the country promising price hikes for electricity, water and other basic services? Which candidate will tell its supporters that 'tough decisions' must be made involving cutbacks in social spending and an end to school meals for the poor? Which candidate will pledge to repeal urban and rural reform measures which grant land and titles to the dispossessed?

It will be extremely difficult for a future president to justify the undoing of citizen power. The Venezuelan people have flexed the muscles of citizenship and will be reluctant go back to sleep. 'The path of democratic legitimacy requires the recovery of truth and the media has a vital role in fulfilling this mission,' said Andrés Izarra, the dissident journalist who confronted his dishonest corporate media employers. Izarra concluded that 'such truth-telling is an essential condition for overcoming the deep social divisions through the acknowledgement of each person as an individual and as a citizen.'[13] Hugo Chávez is faced with an immense political battle based on low blows and dirty tricks. He cannot turn around decades of economic mismanagement in a matter of a few years. Chávez has failed in what can only be described as an impossible task. There is no shame in this. If he is humble enough to acknowledge this truth he may also come to see that his government has sown the seeds of a more permanent revolution. The next phase of this process will not rely on the charisma of a single individual but upon the collective memory and joint action of a people awoken from the slumber of the bayonet, alive now to the certainty that they can reclaim their country from its arrogant elite.

## Postscript

On October 17th 2003, Bolivian President Gonzalo Sánchez de Losada fled to Miami, Florida, forced out of office by a popular uprising against plans to build a gas pipeline that would pump cheap energy to California. The initial protests against the pipeline were greeted with army and police terror which left 76 people dead and five hundred more injured. The repression prompted a wave of mass mobilisations that shut down the country and united social movements in their determination to sack the disgraced leader. The US Government defended

# Scenes from the Bolivarian Revolution

Sánchez de Losada even after his own vice-president and political party had abandoned him, placing themselves once more on the wrong side of history.

In neighbouring Colombia right-wing President Álvaro Uribe staked his political capital on a 15-point referendum that would have cut social spending and reduced the size of congress. Uribe campaigned tirelessly for the referendum, banking on his supposed 70 per cent approval rating to carry through the proposed reforms. On the eve of the vote Uribe warned citizens that if his reform measures were not approved then the country would end up bankrupt like Argentina and the war on terror would be compromised. On October 26th 2003 Colombians overwhelmingly rejected Uribe's referendum as 75 per cent of voters chose to stay at home rather than cast a vote. The referendum agenda required a 25 per cent turnout to secure approval but only two of the fifteen points achieved the required minimum vote. The result was a categorical rejection of Uribe's 'democratic security' project which has curtailed civil liberties and granted sweeping powers to the armed forces. The Uribe administration suffered a further setback the following day when left-wing candidate Luis Eduardo Garzón was elected mayor of Bogotá, defeating Uribe's chosen candidate for the second most important post in the country. The Garzón victory marked a historic shift in Colombia's two-party system which has resisted intruders for 180 years.

The Bolivian uprising and the Colombian vote suggest that voters in the region are fed up with neo-liberal pro-US administrations that have impoverished the people and ceded sovereignty to transnational corporations. In a rare break with tradition, Associated Press ran a story titled 'Venezuelan Recall Campaign Lacks Luster' (November 6, 2003) acknowledging that the recall referendum sought by anti-Chávez forces 'hasn't drummed up much enthusiasm'. Antonio Gil, president of the polling firm Datanalisis, said that Venezuela's opposition lacked

and ideas. 'The fervor is not there,' admitted Gil.
project and there is no leader.'

President Hugo Chávez's political career is far from over.

## Notes

1 *El Nacional,* July 30, 2003.
2 *The Financial Times,* June 13, 2003.
3 *El Universal,* July 15, 2003.
4 *El Nacional,* July 10, 2003.
5 *El Nacional,* August 3, 2003.
6 *The Economist,* June 14, 2003.
7 Personal Communication, Michael A. Lebowitz, August 8, 2003.
8 *El Nacional,* June 28, 2003.
9 *El Nacional,* June 27, 2003.
10 *El Nacional,* July 8, 2003.
11 *El Nacional,* July 12, 2002.
12 Personal interview, July 2002.
13 Izarra's statement to the National Assembly, May 23, 2002.